JEAN NOUVEL
RECENT PROJECT

ジャン・ヌヴェル 最新プロジェクト

204 total pages / English and Japanese text / Size: 300×257mm

RECENT PROJECT SERIES 最新プロジェクト・シリーズ

English and Japanese text / Size: 300×257mm　¥3,800

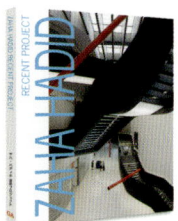
ZAHA HADID
ザハ・ハディド
180 total pages

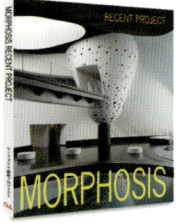
MORPHOSIS
モーフォシス
160 total pages

FRANK GEHRY
フランク・ゲーリー
172 total pages

OMA
OMA
180 total pages

BIG
ビャルケ・インゲルス・グループ
208 total pages

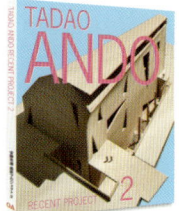
TADAO ANDO 2
安藤忠雄
180 total pages

SOU FUJIMOTO
藤本壮介
192 total pages

表記価格に消費税は含まれておりません。

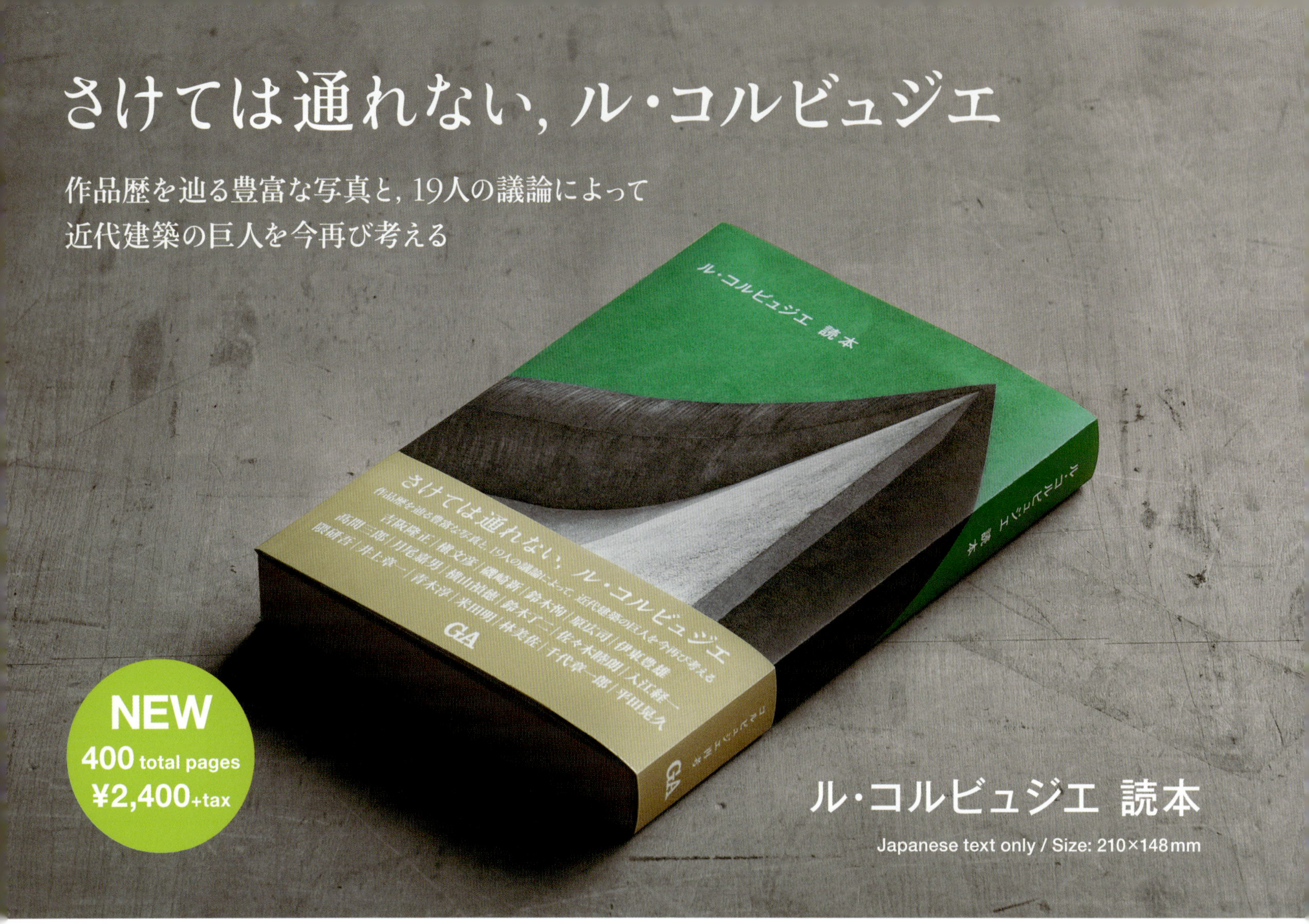

さけては通れない，ル・コルビュジエ

作品歴を辿る豊富な写真と，19人の議論によって
近代建築の巨人を今再び考える

NEW
400 total pages
¥2,400+tax

ル・コルビュジエ 読本
Japanese text only / Size: 210×148mm

建築が生まれる
現場のリアリティ

所内での膨大な検討から様々な協働作業まで
設計の舞台裏を完全ドキュメント

PLOT 04 RYUE NISHIZAWA
西沢立衛：建築のプロセス

［収録作品］
十和田市現代美術館｜豊島美術館
軽井沢千住博美術館｜小豆島の葺田パヴィリオン

［インタヴュー］
西沢立衛の現在形［聞き手：二川由夫］
軽井沢千住博美術館について［聞き手：二川幸夫］

size: 257×182mm｜Japanese text only｜216 total pages　¥2,300+税

GA JAPAN

Global Architecture

日本の新しい優れた現代建築のエッセンスを主に国内に向けて発信する、
隔月刊の建築デザイン専門誌。
建築思想、技術思想を照射しつつ、建築のデザインに迫る本格的建築総合誌です。

最新号

128

座談会：建築家の旅 [インドのコルビュジエに会いに行く]

伊東豊雄×妹島和世×西沢立衛

特集：建築∞政治（序） [現代における「建築と政治」の関係を8人の賢者が語る]
御厨貴，隈研吾，藤村龍至，飯島洋一，蓑原敬，中島岳志，新井清一，鈴木了二

ロングインタヴュー：[駅は建築か!?「場」の理論から考える] 原広司

作品
上州富岡駅／武井誠＋鍋島千恵
日清食品グループ the WAVE／古谷誠章＋竹中工務店

Project
ハノイ市都市鉄道建設計画（二号線）C1〜3／原広司，新徳山駅ビル／内藤廣，白島新駅／CAt

PLOT
「バロックミュージアム・プエブラ」編／伊東豊雄
「中国美術学院博物館」編／隈研吾，「鹿手袋の長屋」編／藤野高志

連載
空間のディテール5「パークドーム熊本」／高橋靗一，インタヴュー：川口衞
現代の建築家 19「磯崎新」／井上章一
二川幸夫の眼 2／鈴木了二
新連載：ロボットはコンピュータの夢をかたちにするか？1／竹中司＋岡部文／アンズスタジオ

GA広場
富士山世界遺産センター（仮称）／編集部
東京藝術大学音楽学部第6ホール改修／中本太郎＋羽鳥達也＋青柳創／日建設計
Ginza natsuno R bld／武井誠＋鍋島千恵，サイクルステーションとりで／中村実・小川達也・小引寛也，
Abre Blanc／藤本壮介＋ニコラ・レネ＋マナル・ラシディ，太田駅北口駅前文化交流施設／平田晃久

208 pages, 64 in color / Japanese text only
¥2,333

MINKA 1955
Japanese Traditional Houses

Edited and Photographed by Yukio Futagawa

144 total pages, 364×257mm, English and Japanese text ¥3,600

GA HOUSES
Key to Abbreviations

ALC	alcove
ARCD	arcade/covered passageway
ART	art room
ATL	atelier
ATR	atrium
ATT	attic
AV	audio-visual room
BAL	balcony
BAR	bar
BK	breakfast room
BR	bedroom
BRG	bridge/catwalk
BTH	bathroom
BVD	belvedere/lookout
CAR	carport/car shelter
CH	children's room
CEL	cellar
CL	closet/walk-in closet
CLK	cloak
CT	court
D	dining room
DEN	den
DK	deck
DN	stairs-down
DRK	darkroom
DRS	dressing room/wardrobe
DRW	drawing room
E	entry
ECT	entrance court
EH	entrance hall
EV	elevator
EXC	exercise room
F	family room
FPL	fireplace
FYR	foyer
GAL	gallery
GDN	garden
GRG	garage
GRN	greenhouse
GST	guest room/guest bedroom
GZBO	gazebo
H	hall
HK	house keeper
ING	inglenook
K	kitchen
L	living room
LBR	library
LBY	lobby
LDRY	laundry
LFT	loft
LGA	loggia
LGE	lounge
LWL	light well
MBR	master bedroom
MBTH	master bathroom
MECH	mechanical
MLTP	multipurpose room
MSIC	music room
MUD	mud room
OF	office
P	porch/portico
PAN	pantry/larder
PLY	playroom
POOL	swimming pool/pool/pond
PT	patio
RE	rear entry
RT	roof terrace
SHW	shower
SIT	sitting room
SHOP	shop
SKY	skylight
SL	slope/ramp
SLP	sleeping loft
SNA	sauna
STD	studio
STDY	study
ST	staircase/stair hall
STR	storage/storeroom
SUN	sunroom/sun parlor/solarium
SVE	service entry
SVYD	service yard
TAT	tatami room/tea ceremony room
TER	terrace
UP	stairs-up
UTL	utility room
VD	void/open
VRA	veranda
VSTB	vestibule
WC	water closet
WRK	workshop/work room

表記価格に消費税は含まれておりません。

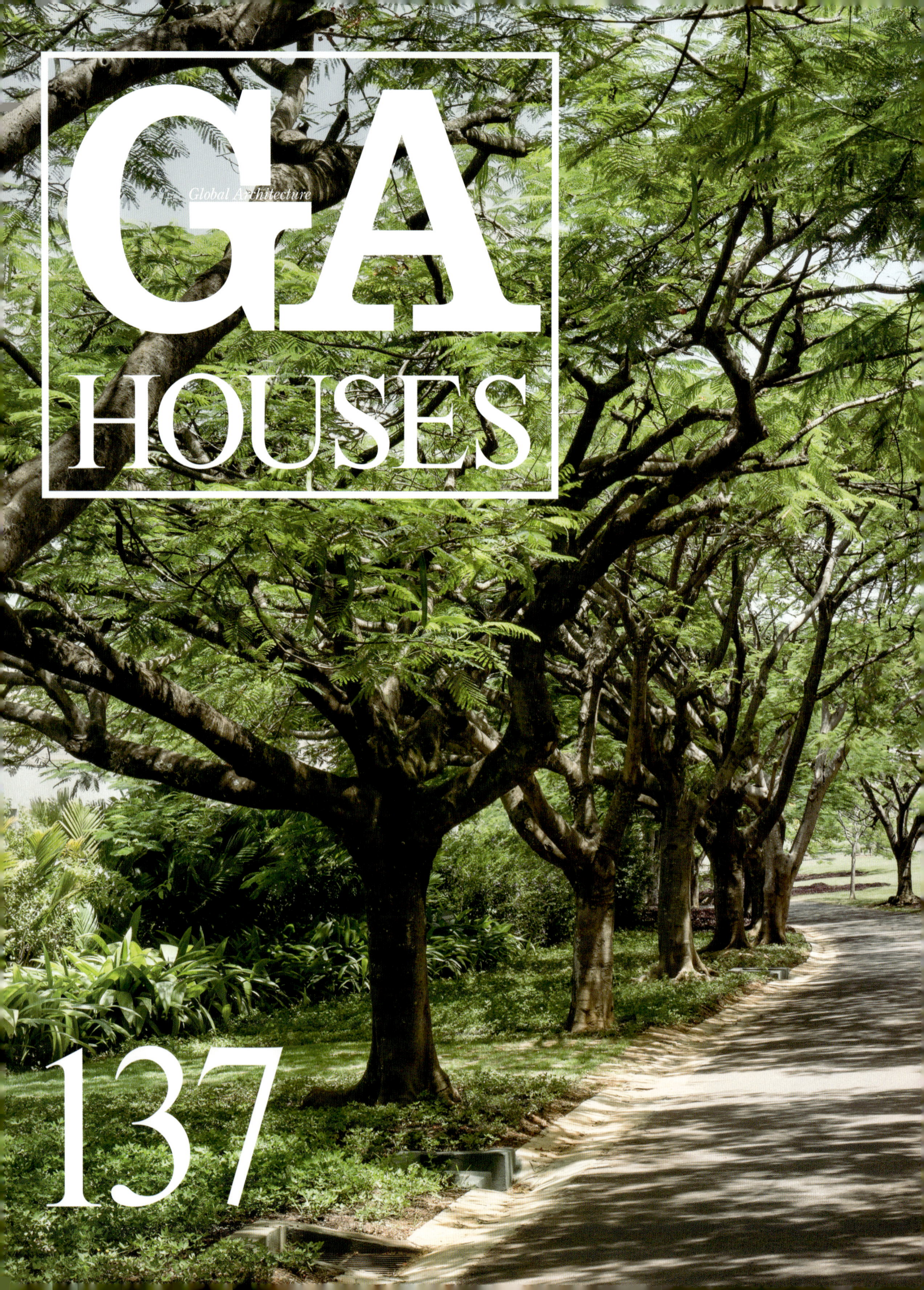

Contents／目次

- 8 **Keisuke Maeda: Cosmic**
  前田圭介：群峰の森
- 36 **Studio MK27: P House**
  スタジオMK27：Pハウス
- 50 **Studio MK27: Lee House**
  スタジオMK27：リー・ハウス
- 62 **SPBR Arquitetos: House in Ribeirão Preto**
  spbrアルキテートス：ヒベイラン・プレートの家
- 74 **SPBR Arquitetos: House and Studio in Orlandia**
  spbrアルキテートス：オルランジャのスタジオ＋ハウス
- 90 **Hironaka Ogawa: Bellows House**
  小川博央：Bellows House

100	Ryo Abe: Perfil
	安部良：まちのPerfil
110	Marcos Acayaba: Helio Olga House
	マルコス・アカヤバ：エリオ・オルガ・ハウス
124	Gesto Arquitetura: Jatobá Residence
	ジェスト・アルキテットゥーラ：ジャトバ・ハウス
138	Reinach Mendonça Arquitetos: MG Residence
	レイナッハ／メンドンサ・アルキテートス：MGハウス
148	Andrade Morettin: FS House
	アンドラージ／モレティン：FSハウス

《世界の住宅》137
発行・編集：二川由夫

2014年5月23日発行
エーディーエー・エディタ・トーキョー
東京都渋谷区千駄ヶ谷3-12-14
電話 (03)3403-1581(代)
ファックス (03)3497-0649
E-mail: info@ga-ada.co.jp
http://www.ga-ada.co.jp

ロゴタイプ・デザイン：細谷巖

印刷・製本：図書印刷株式会社

取次店：
トーハン, 日販, 大阪屋
栗田出版販売, 西村書店, 中央社
太洋社, 鍬谷書店

禁無断転載
ISBN978-4-87140-085-5 C1352

GA HOUSES 137
Publisher/Editor: Yoshio Futagawa

Published in May 2014
©A.D.A. EDITA Tokyo Co., Ltd.
3-12-14 Sendagaya, Shibuya-ku, Tokyo,
151-0051 Japan
Tel. (03)3403-1581
Fax. (03)3497-0649
E-mail: info@ga-ada.co.jp
http://www.ga-ada.co.jp

Logotype Design: Gan Hosoya

Printed in Japan by
Tosho Printing Co., Ltd.

All rights reserved.
Copyright of Photographs:
©GA photographers
All drawings are provided by
architects except as noted.

Cover: Cosmic by Keisuke Maeda
pp.4-5: Lee House by Studio MK27
pp.6-7: FS House by Andrade Morettin
Photos by Yoshio Futagawa
English translation: Lisa Tani (p.10),
Satoko Hirata (p.92), Erica Sakai (p.101)
和訳：原田勝之 (p.68, p.79, p.135, p.159),
上野黄 (p.49, p.53, pp.116-117, p.143)

KEISUKE MAEDA
COSMIC
Osaka, Japan
Photos: Yoshio Futagawa

West elevation: view from approach 西面：アプローチから見る

Dwelling is to put oneself in an interactive environmental domain that surrounds humans and other living creatures. There unfold various activities to which living creatures engage themselves for survival. Further expansion of such domain will surely lead us to view the totality of environment as a dwelling as it stretches unsegmented from city to forest and sea and finally from the earth into outer space. The ever-changing ways of living things such as humans and plants, land topographies or climatic conditions all remind us that nothing in our world stays the same forever. My interest lies in the rich spatial domain in which one may perceive in the course of daily life such changes of nature that are the very heartbeats of the earth.

In this project the focus is on the relationship of borders derived from mutual interaction with natural environment that surrounds this site sitting on a hill. Instead of gathering up a crowd of spaces within the topography or climate by making use of wall/roof elements, it rather involves a domain generated by screens like clouds that shield sunlight and moonlight. In other words this infinitely expansive totality with no boundaries bases itself on the principles of architecture while it generates a certain domain within topological and climatic conditions. While wisps of clouds overlap in layers, exposure and depth of light penetrating through mountain peaks into the valley define the atmospheric void as a domain for a place of living. These screens that flow from east to west not only work as eaves that shield direct sunlight during summer but also serve as constituents along with subtle light tones, sway in the wind, atmospheric condition, nature's sounds and scents and physical sense of distance that highlight the diversity of spatial domains through the seasons. The state of the spot generated by screens becomes the place of living that paraphrases the topography through various actions, rather than being a space specialized in particular functions. The architecture is like a village as it breaks free from borders defined by natural relationships, and is also like a mountain ridge with its layers of mountain peaks. With an ever transforming outline, it will continue to blur into the landscape.

Keisuke Maeda

South elevation of annex wing　アネックス棟の南面

South elevation

West elevation S=1:120

View from northwest: main wing　北西より見る：メイン棟

View from garden on northeast　北東側の庭より見る

　住むとは人間あるいは生物を取り囲みインタラクティブな環境領域に身を置くことである。そこには生物の生きていく多様な活動があり，その領域を拡張していくと都市から森や海へ，そして地球から宇宙へと分節されることのない環境の総体を住まいとして捉えることができるのではないだろうか。人間や植物など生命あるもの，そして大地の地形や大気の状態など刻々と変化し続ける様は，この世に常住不変はないことを気付かせてくれる。そのような地球の鼓動である自然のうつろいを日常の中で意識できる豊かな空間領域に興味がある。

　今回，小高い丘にある敷地周辺の自然環境との相互作用から生成される境界の関係性について考えた。それは，地形や大気の中で壁／屋根の要素によって空間の取り巻きをつくり出すのではなく，陽光や月光を遮る雲のような覆いによってつくり出す領域である。つまり地形や大気の状態に，ある領域をつくりながらも総体としてはどこまでも広がる境界のない建築原理である。ひとすじのたなびく雲が重層的に織り重なり，群峰のような谷間から差し込む光の露出や深度によって，大気のがらんどうは居場所としての領域を顕在化させる。この東西にたなびく覆いは夏季の直射光を遮蔽する軒の働きから始まり，光の微妙な階調，風によるゆらぎや大気の状態，自然の奏でる音や香り，身体的距離感など，四季を通じて多様な空間領域を彩る構成要素となる。覆いによって生成された場の状態は特定の機能に特化する空間ではなく様々な行為によってパラフレイズしていく地形の居場所となる。自然の関係性から導かれる境界を解き放つ建築は小さな集落のようなスケールから，峰の稜線を連ねていく尾根のようなスケールまで輪郭を変容しながら風景へと滲んでいく。

（前田圭介）

Evening view from south 南側夕景

Garage of annex wing　アネックス棟ガレージ

Entrance approach between two garages　2つのガレージに挟まれた玄関への路地

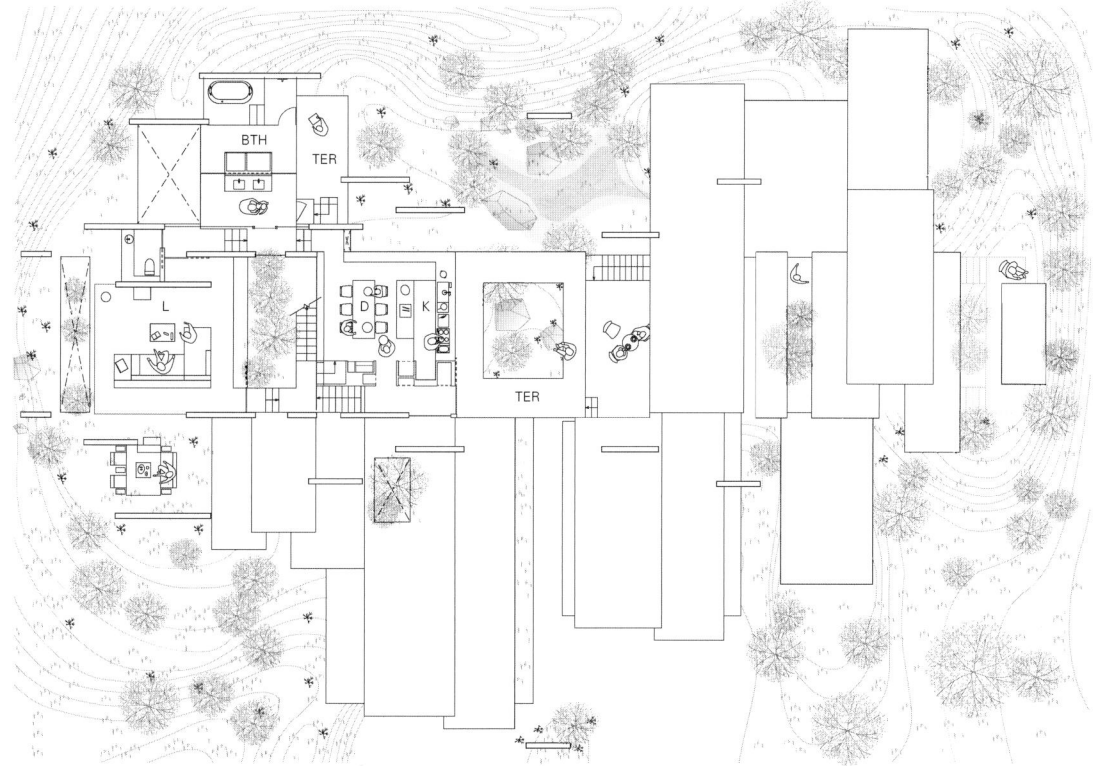
Second floor

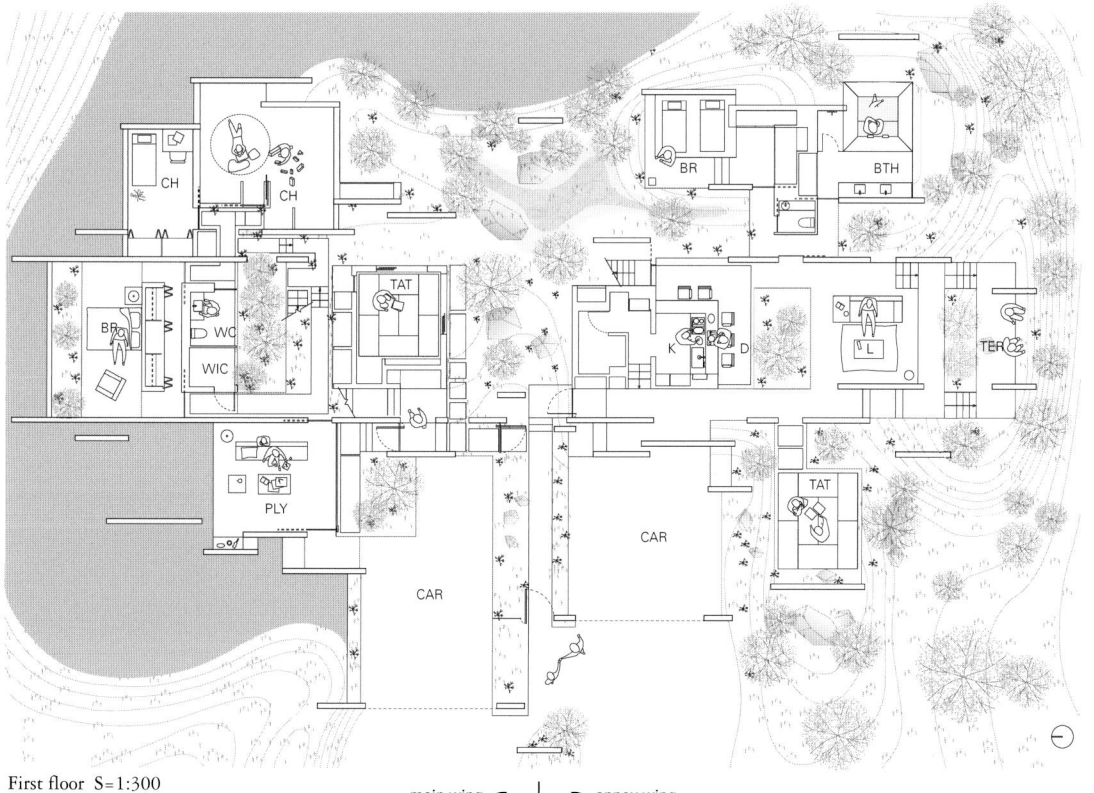
First floor S=1:300

main wing ← | → annex wing

Architects: UID—Keisuke Maeda, principal-in-charge; Hiroyuki Ueda, project team
Consultants: Konishi Structural Engineers—Yasutaka Konishi, Takeshi Kaneko, structural; Toshiya Ogino Environment Design Office—Toshiya Ogino, Minoru Nishikawa, Shota Ogino, landscape
General Contractor:
Makoto Construction Co., Ltd
—Hisahiro Shimizu, Hajime Matsumoto, Mamoru Yamaguchi, Masahiro Ikegami
Structural system: reinforced concrete, steel frame
Major materials: resin mortar, finishing photocatalyst paint, exterior;
rough puttying + EP, organic quality sand-coated wall-formed spray; (wall, ceiling), black granite stone (floor), interior
Site area: 2,107.88 m²
Building area: 611.51 m²
Total floor area: 573.17 m²
Design: 2010-12
Construction: 2012-14

Entrance approach 玄関への路地

East garden: view from annex wing toward main wing 東庭：アネックス棟よりメイン棟を見る

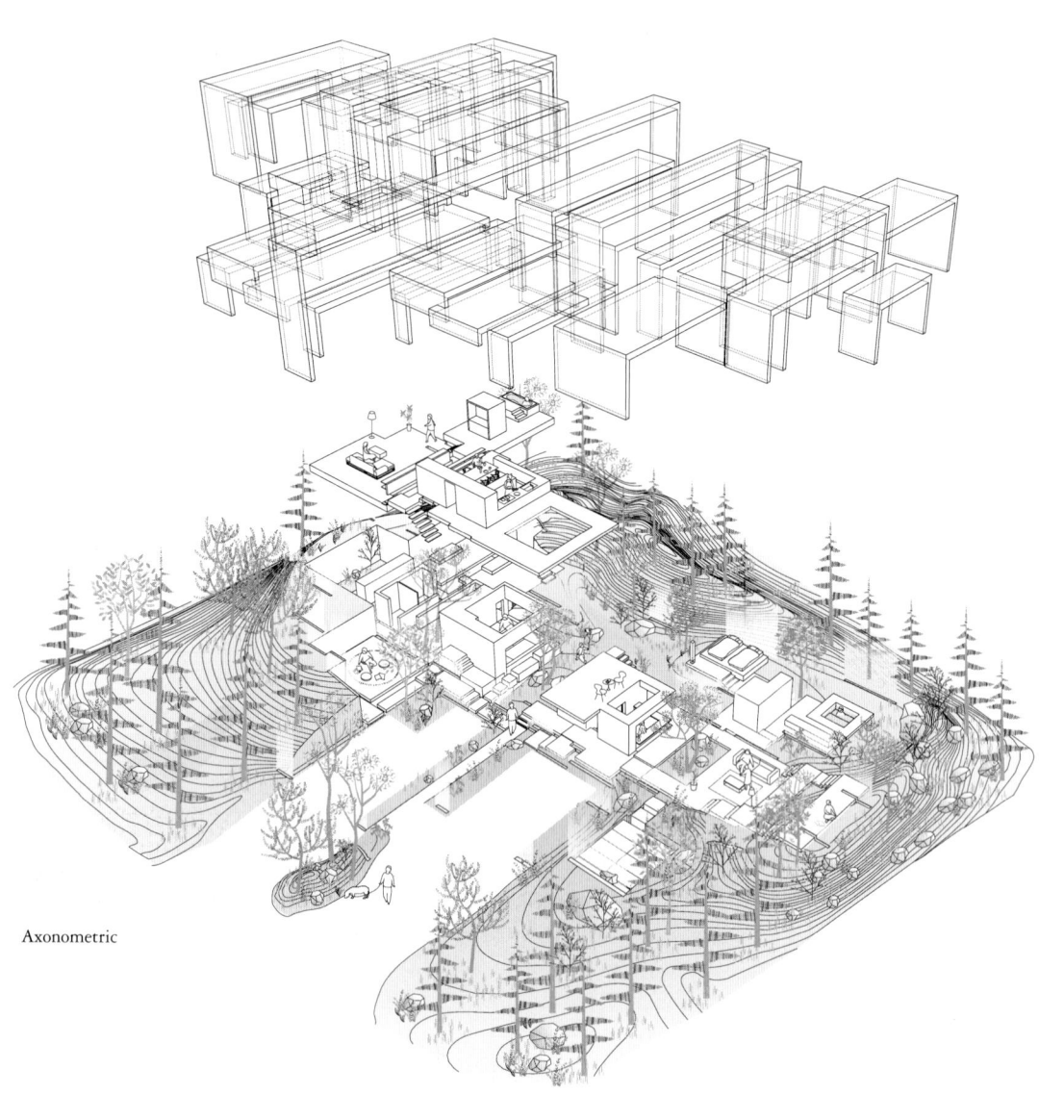

Axonometric

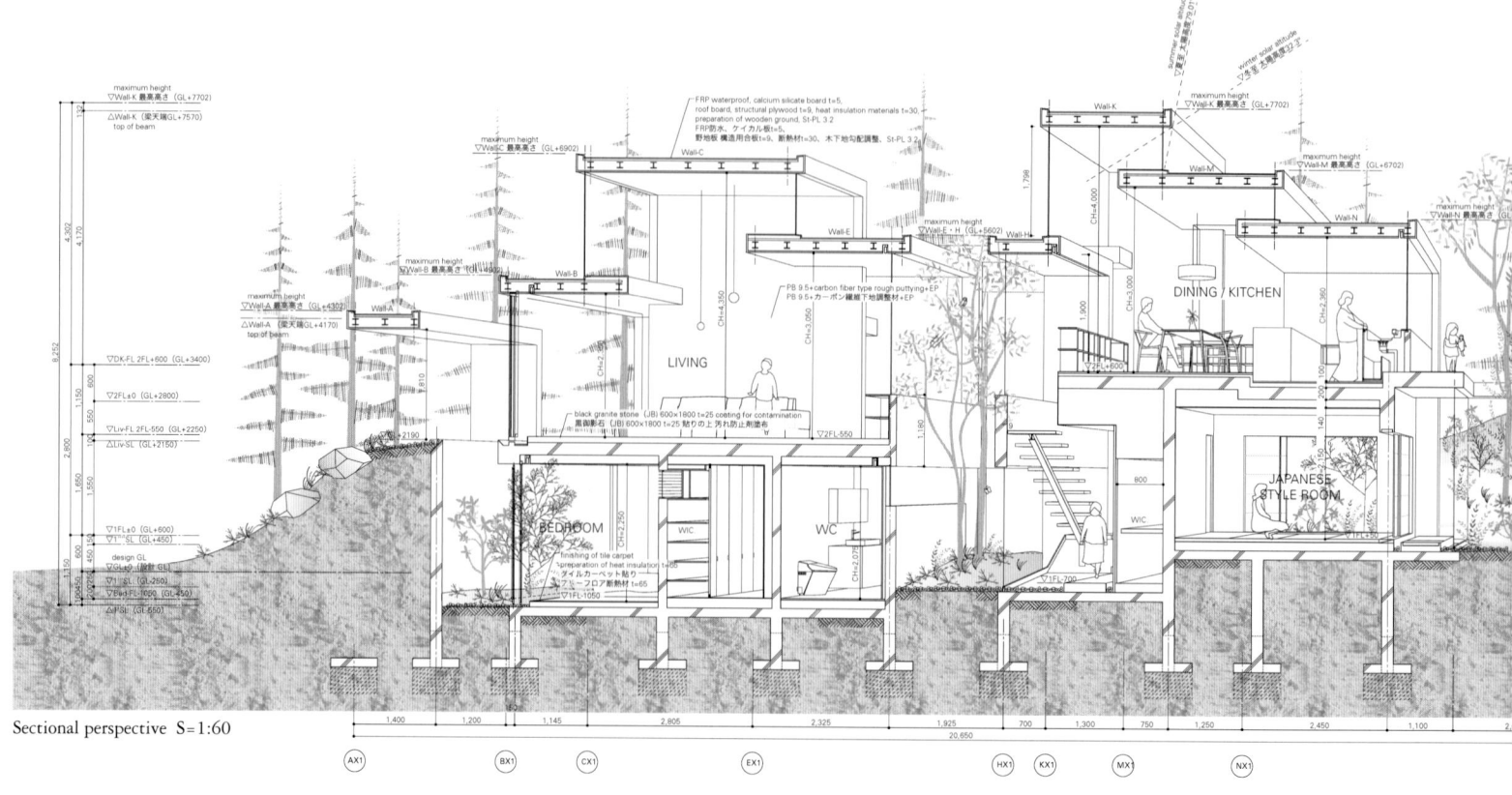

Sectional perspective S=1:60

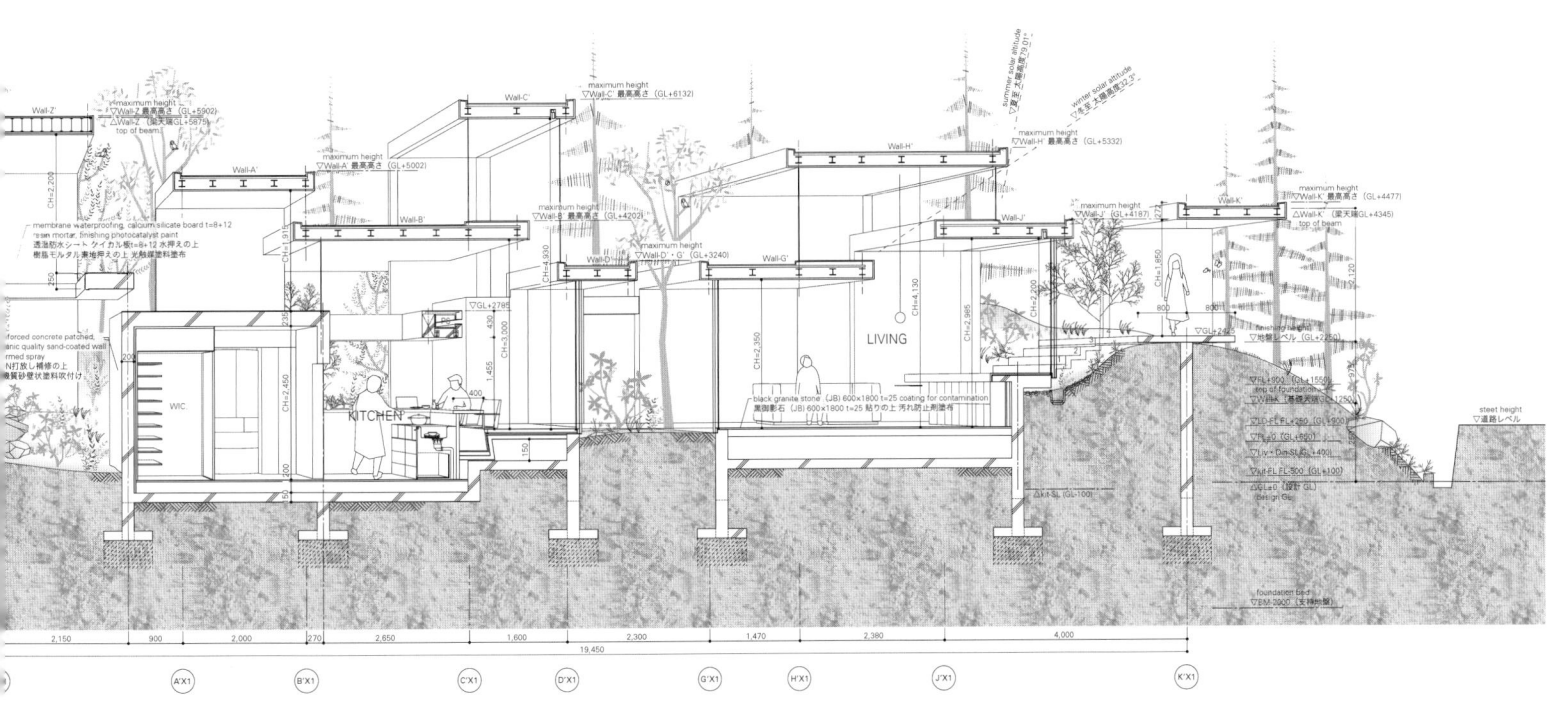

View toward entrance approach: entrance of annex wing on left　路地を見返す：左にアネックス棟の玄関

Annex wing: view from entrance　アネックス棟：玄関から見る

Annex wing: view from dining room toward living room　アネックス棟：食堂より居間を見る

Living room of annex wing アネックス棟居間

Bathroom on southeast corner of annex wing アネックス棟南東隅の浴室

Annex wing: dining room (left), courtyard and living room (right)　アネックス棟：食堂（左），居間と中庭（右）

Bedroom of annex wing　アネックス棟寝室

Bedroom: view toward north　寝室：北を見る

Keisuke Maeda / Cosmic　25

View from garden between bedroom (right) and dining room (left). Stairs to terrace between two wings
寝室（右）と食堂（左）の間の庭より見る。階段は2棟の間のテラスへ続く

Tatami room on southwest corner 南西隅部の和室

View from tatami room toward living/dining area 和室より居間／食堂側を見る

Keisuke Maeda / Cosmic

Terrace and courtyard between main wing (left) and annex wing (right)　メイン棟（左）とアネックス棟（右）の間にあるテラスと中庭

View of main wing from terrace テラスからメイン棟を見る

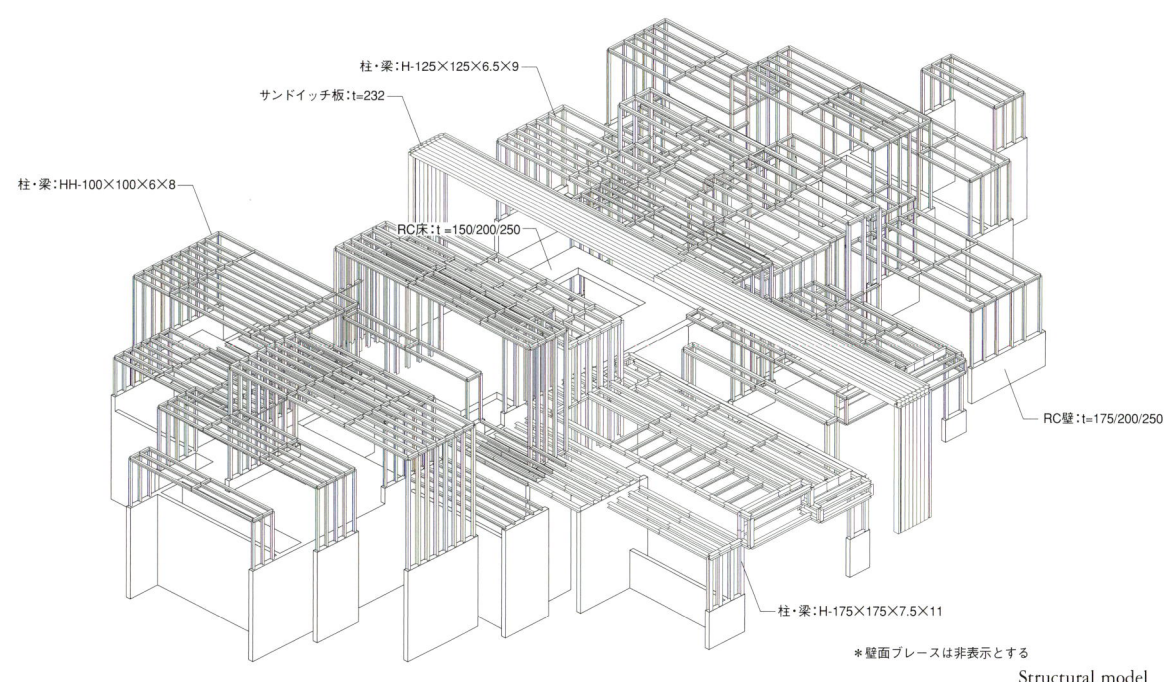

柱・梁:H-125×125×6.5×9
サンドイッチ板:t=232
柱・梁:HH-100×100×6×8
RC床:t=150/200/250
RC壁:t=175/200/250
柱・梁:H-175×175×7.5×11

＊壁面ブレースは非表示とする
Structural model

Keisuke Maeda / Cosmic   29

Staircase of main wing: dining room on right メイン棟の階段室：右に食堂

Dining room/kitchen of main wing メイン棟食堂／台所

Eastern corridor of main wing　メイン棟，東側の廊下

Bathroom on second floor of main wing　メイン棟 2 階の浴室

View from terrace toward corridor of main wing. Kitchen on right
テラスよりメイン棟の廊下を見る。右は台所

Living room of main wing: looking north メイン棟居間：北を見る

Living room of main wing: looking west メイン棟居間：西を見る

Outdoor living room on west of indoor living 居間西隣にある屋外の居間

△▷Staircase to dining/living area of main wing　メイン棟食堂／居間へ至る階段

Children's room　子供室

Bedroom on north　北側の寝室

Tatami room of main wing: looking south メイン棟和室：南を見る

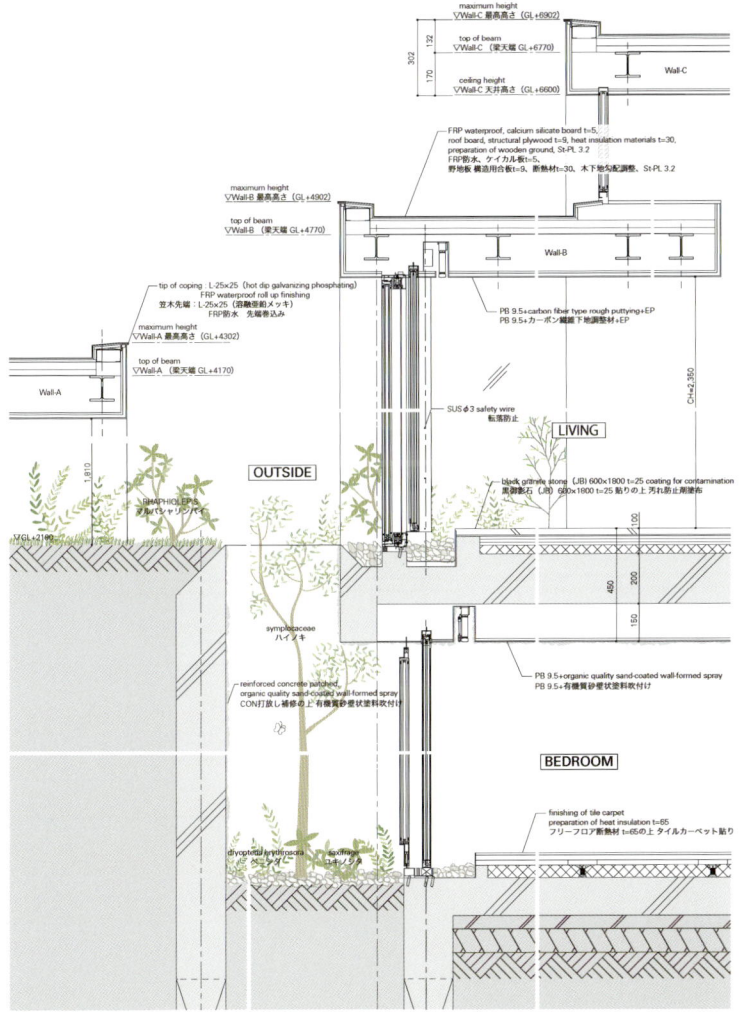

Sectional detail (main wing) S=1:30

Corridor beside children's room 子供室横の廊下

STUDIO MK27
P HOUSE
São Paulo, Brazil

Photos: Yoshio Futagawa

View from street on north 北側接道より見る

The Pinheiro house is a puzzle game. Rotating three volumes around one nucleus generated not only a particular spatial dynamic, but also different visual relations between empty and full, between the private and semiprivate areas and the view of the city.

The site is located on the other side of the Pinheiros River, one of the main rivers that define and cut into the city of São Paulo, in an essentially residential neighborhood, Morumbi. From there it is possible to see the entire valley filled with gardened houses, the river and, on the other margin, another hill, the corporate area of the city drawing the metropolitan skyline with its typical skyscrapers.

The program boasts three floors: a garden, a terrace with fireplace and barbecue, home theater, dining and living rooms, washroom, kitchen, four bedrooms, office and family room. In the basement: a garage, laundry room, utility rooms and a gym. The nucleus of the circulation is made of a continuous staircase joined in a structural wall. This block, which organizes the structure and distributes the fluxes, is the pivot around which the boxes revolve.

The volumes are developed to create constant and distinct relations between the inner and outer spaces. The bedrooms on the second floor look out to the pool and take advantage of the deck above the roof of the living and dining rooms. The box comprising the bedrooms projects outwards over both sides of the first box. From one side, the cantilever determines the main entrance of the house and, on the other, it shades the terrace.

The spiral movement continues with the third box, supported by the second and projecting outwards over the first. It shades the window of the master bedroom and part of the deck while, simultaneously, creates new visual relations with the other bedrooms and the deck.

All of the boxes are bare concrete frames. The living room and the bedrooms have their sides closed by freijó wooden folding panels, which filter the light and allow for permanent crossed ventilation. The family room, on the top floor is enclosed by glass, to preserve the view.

The result strengthens interactions, the crossing of eye views and vectors through the garden: eyes that see the view and the treetops around the pool, eyes that are turned back to the house itself, its volume and, above all else, to its own life.

Garden view from east 東より庭を見る

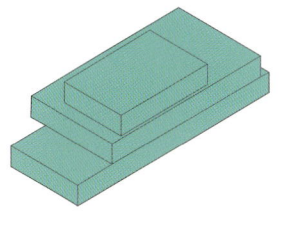

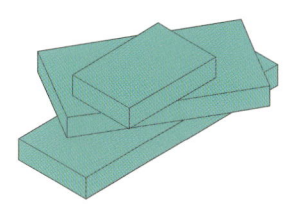

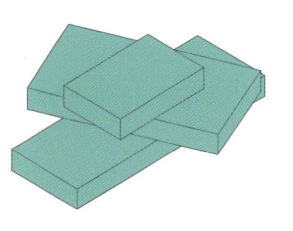

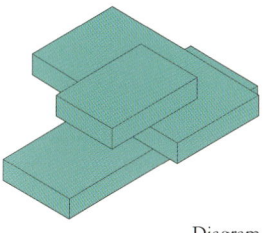

Diagram

Studio MK27 / P House 39

Entrance 玄関

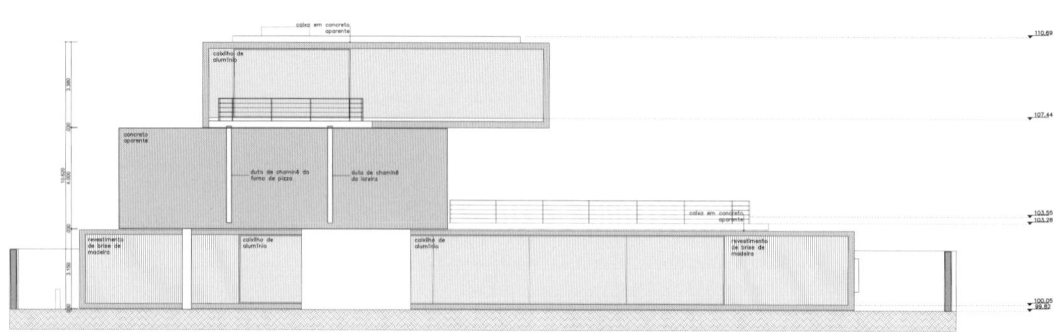

South elevation

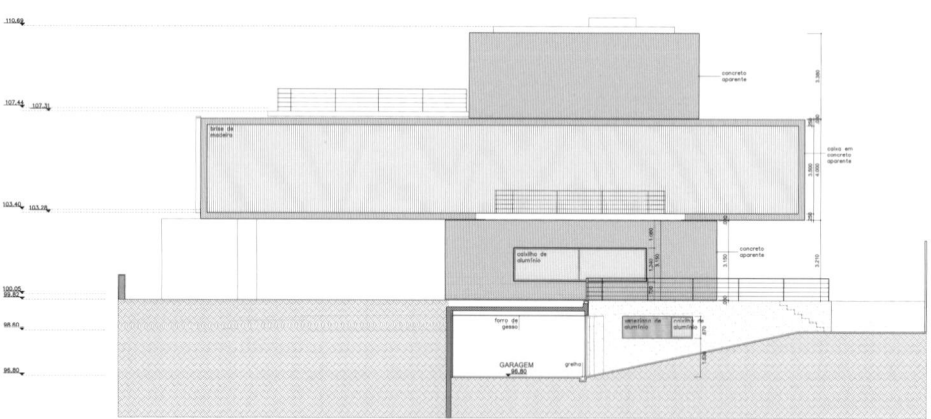

East elevation

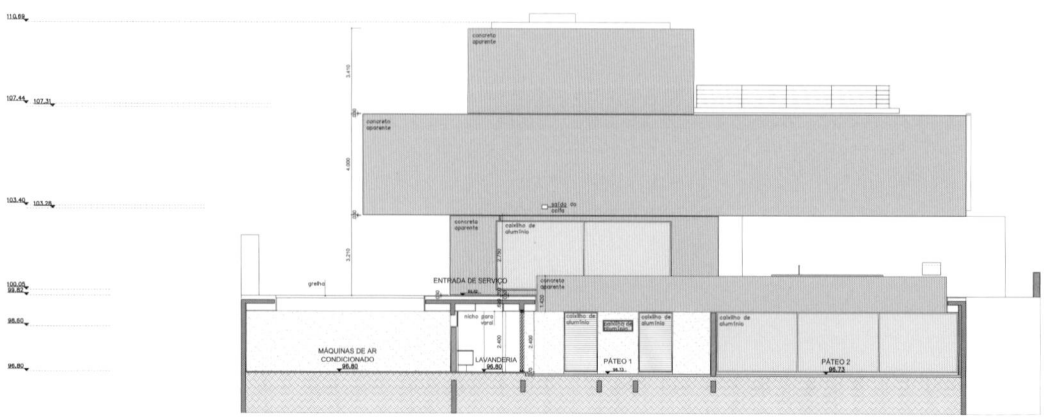

West elevation S=1:300

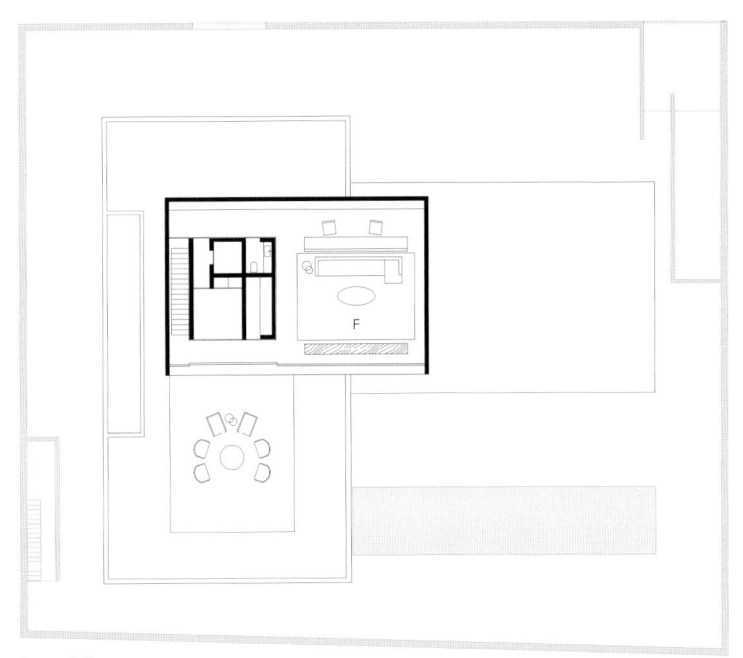

Second floor

First floor

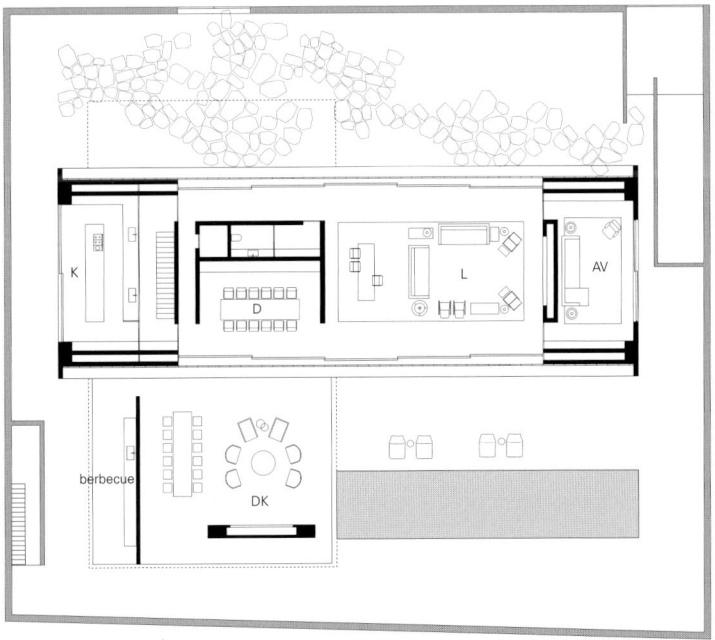

Ground floor S=1:400

Studio MK27 / P House

View toward living/dining room. Deck on left 居間／食堂を見る。左はデッキ

Dining room 食堂

Living room 居間

Corner of living room 居間の一角

View from deck toward garden. Wooden folding panels on left
デッキより庭を見る。左は木製折戸

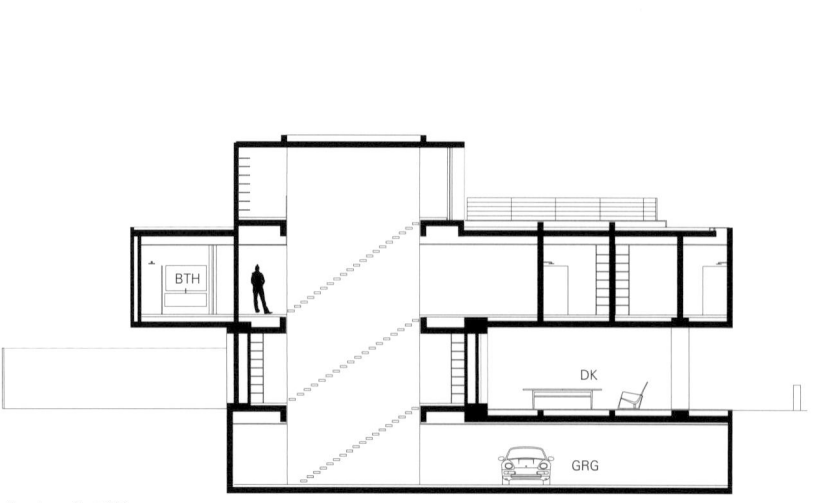

Section S=1:300

Deck デッキ

Garden on entrance side. Living room on left 玄関脇の庭。左は居間

Terrace on first floor: view from east 2階テラス：東より見る

Master bedroom 主寝室

Corridor 廊下

Master bathroom 主浴室

Second floor: view toward family room　3階：家族室を見る

Family room　家族室

Architect: Studio MK27—Marcio Kogan, principal-in-charge; Lair Reis, co-architect; Diana Radomysler, interior design; Andrea Macruz, Samanta Cafardo, Renata Furlanetto, project team
Collaborators: Carolina Castroviejo, Carlos Costa, Laura Guedes, Mariana Simas, Oswaldo Pessano, Suzana Glogowski
Architectural collaborator: Fernanda Neiva
Consultant: Renata Tilli, landscape; Studio MK27, lighting
General contractor: CPA—Henriques Ferreiro, Luiz Schwartz, Rafael Canto Porto
Structural system: reinforced concrete
Major materials: concrete, wood, glass, aluminium, limestone
Site area: 1,240 m²
Built area: 773 m²
Design: 2007
Construction: 2012

Family room　家族室

　ピニェイロ・ハウスはまるでパズルゲームのような住宅である。ある一つの点を軸にとり三つのヴォリュームを回転させることで空間的なダイナミズムが生まれるだけでなく、何もない空間と満ちた空間の視覚的な関係性や、あるいはプライベートとセミプライベート、そして街への眺めといったものも生まれる。

　敷地はサンパウロ市の大きな川の一つで、市内を切り込むように流れるピニェイロス川の都心部と反対側、モルンビという古くからの住宅地にある。そこからは谷いっぱいに建つ庭付きの家や川が見渡せ、また川向こうの丘には都会のスカイラインを描く超高層ビル群を見ることができる。

　住宅は全部で3層から成っており、庭、暖炉とバーベキューができるテラス、ホームシアター、ダイニングルーム、リビングルーム、トイレ、キッチン、四つの寝室、書斎、そして家族室が設けられている。地下にはガレージ、洗濯室、ユーティリティ・ルームとジムがある。動線部となる階段室は連続した階段で各階を繋ぎ、また構造壁とつながっている。この中心のブロックは各箱を回転させる中心軸で構造と各所へのスムーズな動線を確保する。

　各箱のヴォリュームは不変的かつ異質な関係性を外と中の空間につくりだすように決められた。2階のベッドルームはプールに開き、リビングとダイニング上部の屋上デッキに出ることもできる。ベッドルームのある箱は1階の箱の上に両端をはみ出すようにして載っている。それによってできるキャンチレバーの一方が正面玄関の空間をつくり、もう一方はデッキの上部に張り出している。

　三つ目の箱も同様に回転させ、2階の箱に支えられながら1階の箱の上にせり出している。これによって主寝室とデッキの一部へ落ちる日光を遮り、同時にその他の寝室とそのテラスに対して新しい視覚的関係性をもたらす。

　箱はすべて打ち放しのコンクリートフレームである。リビングとベッドルームはラウレム（ムラサキ科の植物）の木でつくられた格子窓で閉じることができ、通風と採光を確保する。一番上の箱の家族室はガラスで閉じられ、部屋からの景色が確保されている。

　このプロジェクトでは、結果として庭を介したベクトルと視線の交わりが生まれ、その相互関係が強められたと言って良い。それはプールの上で揺れる木や景色を眺めることであったり、住宅そのものや、あるいは特にそこでの日常生活を見返すことであったりもする。

STUDIO MK27
LEE HOUSE
Porto Feliz, São Paulo, Brazil

View from west 西より見る

Ground floor S=1:400

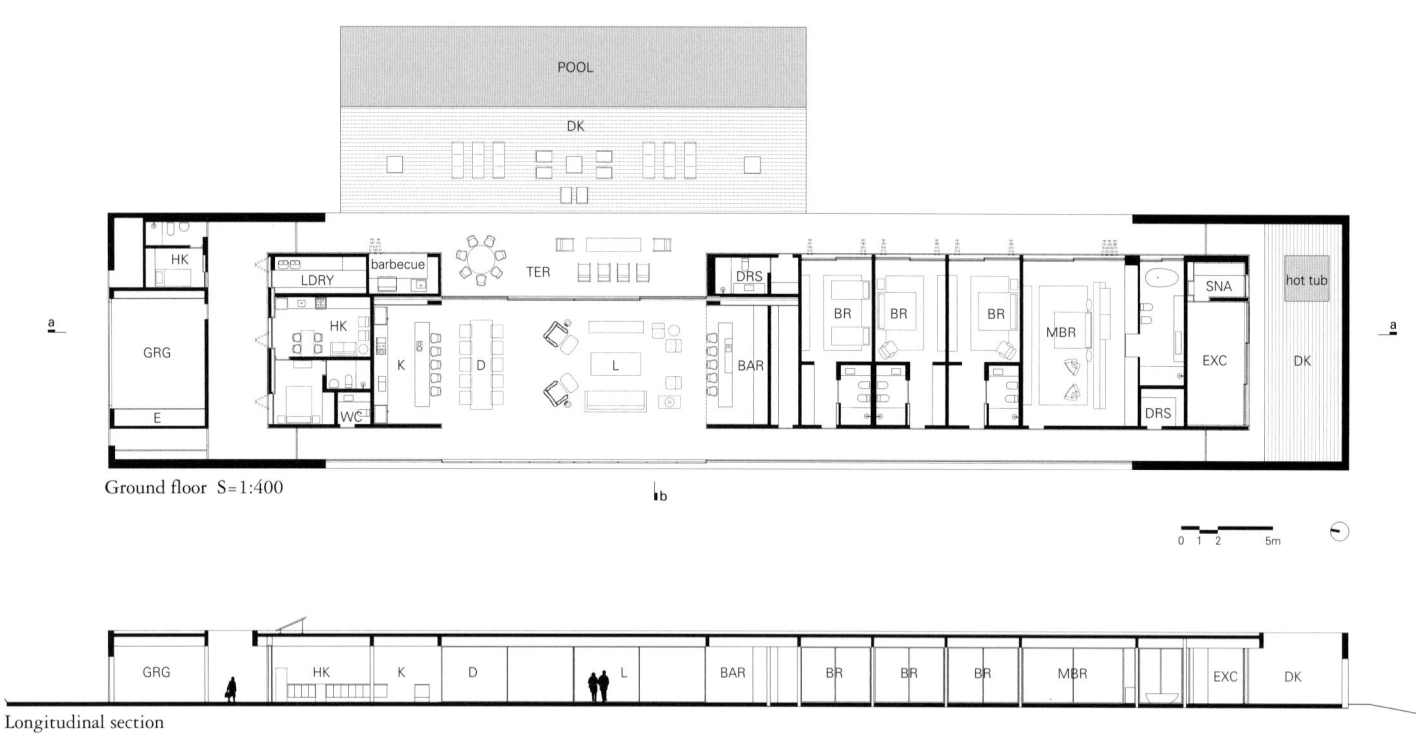

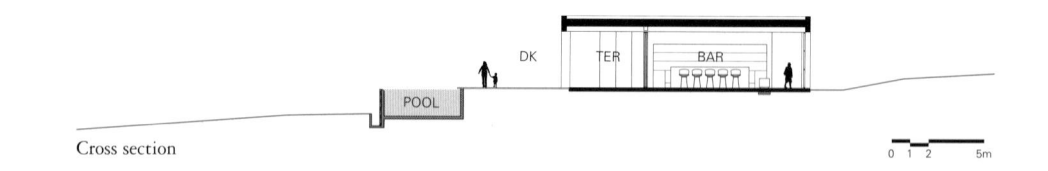

Longitudinal section

Cross section

With the facade radically horizontal, the Lee House is organized in a single volume ground-floor site. All of the rooms therefore, establish a strong relationship with the external, opening out to the garden. The spatial continuity with the living room is larger: all of the windows are recessed creating an extension of the external space, with a large veranda. The living room then prolongs the pool deck and crosses to the other side of the lot.

These solutions are fit for the climate, the interior of the State of São Paulo, in the Brazilian southeast, which has elevated temperatures almost every day of the year. Strategies of traditional ambient comfort of vernacular architecture and even Brazilian modern was used. The living room has cross-ventilation, which greatly lowers the internal temperature and the other rooms are protected by wooden muxarabis panels placed on sliding doors which filter the sun without removing the ventilation.

The front veranda is delimited by a foyer in the facade revealing two wooden boxes divided by the social area. The kitchen opens to the living room, encrusted in one of the boxes that hold the utility areas. The bar opens out to the social area and is contained in the box that holds the bedroom as well. At the end of the corridor of the bedrooms, which can also be accessed from the outside of the house, there is a spa delimited by external walls and composed by a gym room, a sauna and a small outdoor hot tub encircled by the deck.

Besides the wood of the wooden boxes, the house is clad by white mortar and the internal patio of the spa is encircled by stones. The few materials used by the Lee house and the simple organization of the program create a minimalist atmosphere that extends from the outer to the inner areas of the house.

West elevation

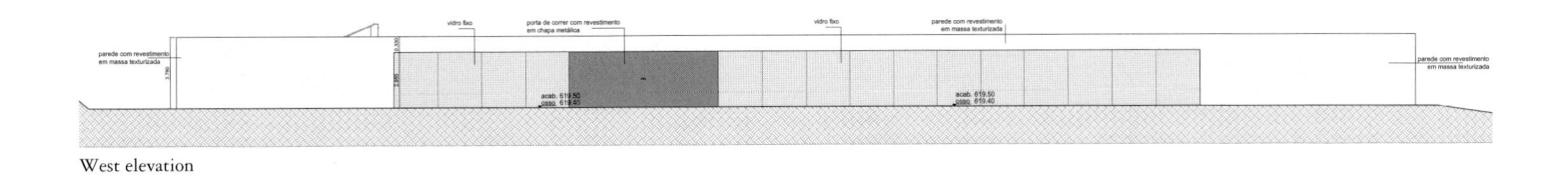

East elevation

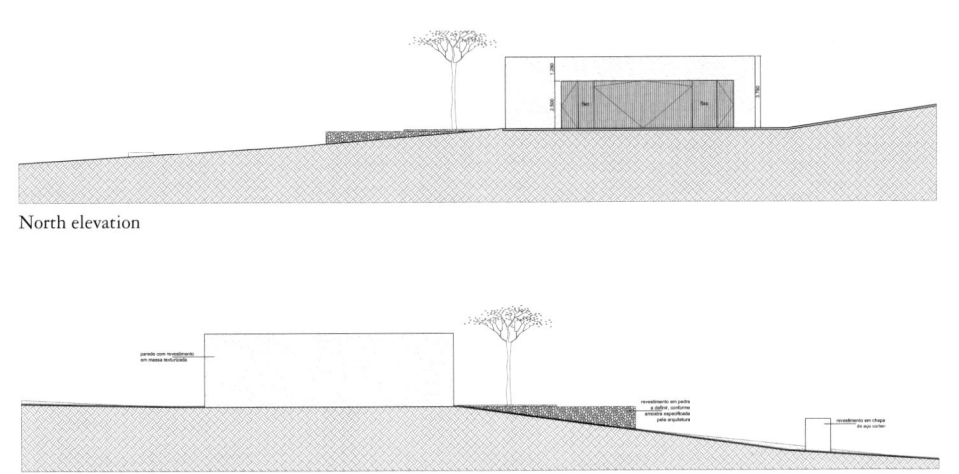

North elevation

South elevation S=1:400

　まっすぐ水平なファサードを持つリー・ハウスは地面の上にヴォリュームが一つ置かれただけの平屋の住宅である。したがってすべての部屋は庭へと開き，外部に対して強い関係を築いている。空間的な連続性は特にリビングルームにおいて強く，大きなベランダをつくるように窓はすべてセットバックして設けられ，外部空間と連続している。またプールデッキがリビングルームへとつながり，そのまま敷地の反対側にまで伸びている。

　ブラジル南東のサンパウロ州の地域では1年を通して毎日のように気温が上がるため，このような手法がこの地方の住宅の屋内環境によく適している。ヴァナキュラー建築や，あるいはブラジルのモダン建築においてもこの屋内環境を快適に保つ伝統的な手法は用いられている。リビングルームは通風が確保され，その他の部屋も含めて徐々に室温が下がるようになっている。その他の部屋には格子状の1枚扉があり，通風を確保しながら日光を遮るフィルターの役割を果たしている。

　正面のベランダはパブリック・エリアを挟む二つの木の箱のホワイエで規定されている。キッチンはリビングルームに対して開かれており，ユーティリティ・エリアを内包する箱の一角を占める。バーはパブリック・エリアに面しており，これもベッドルームの箱に組み込まれている。ベッドルームの廊下へは家の外からも入ることができ，そのつきあたりには外壁が周囲をめぐり，ジムやサウナ，そしてデッキで囲まれた小さなホットタブなどで構成されたスパがある。

　木の箱の木材に加えて家の外装は白いモルタルで仕上げられ，スパの中庭は石貼り。リー・ハウスはわずかな素材でつくられ，またシンプルな諸室の配置が，外から中へと連続する環境においてミニマルに表現されている。

Studio MK27 / Lee House　53

View from east over swimming pool 東側のプール越しに見る

Swimming pool プール

View from terrace toward swimming pool　テラスからプールを見る

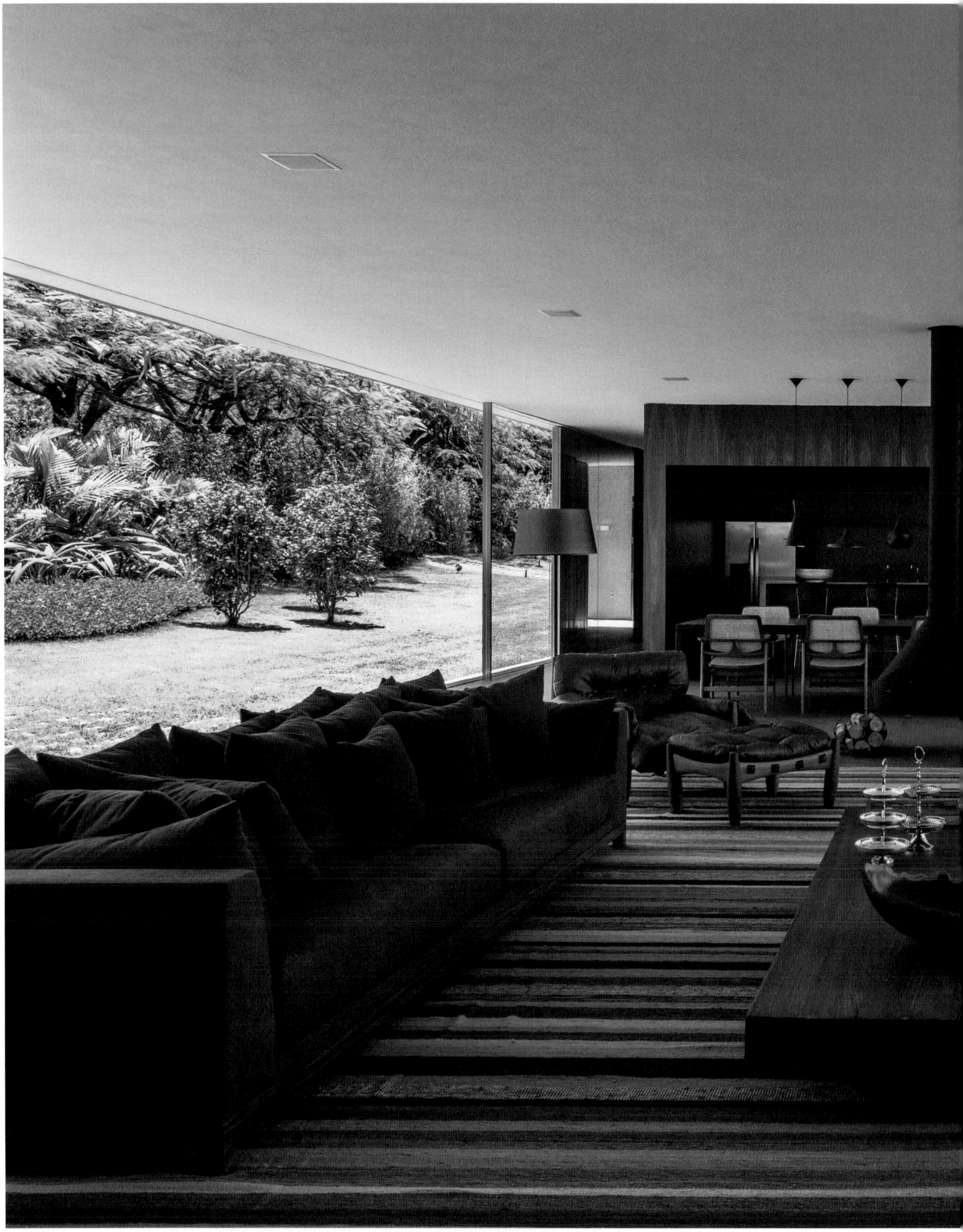

Living room 居間

Dining room 食堂

Living room with sun-shading panels 日除けをした状態の居間

Living room: looking west　居間：西を見る

Corridor: view toward deck on south　廊下：南側のテラスを見る

Corridor 廊下

Closet of master bedroom 主寝室のクローゼット

Master bedroom 主寝室

Architect: Studio MK27—Marcio Kogan, principal-in-charge; Eduardo Glycerio, co-architect; Diana Radomysler, interior design; Gabriel Kogan, Lair Reis, Renata Furlanetto, Samanta Cafardo, Suzana Glogowski, project team
Collaborators: Carolina Castroviejo, Maria Cristina Motta, Mariana Simas, Oswaldo Pessano
Consultant: Benedicts Engenharia—Eduardo Duprat, structural; Eduardo Chalabi, Ricardo Ariza, technical drawings; Gil Fialho, landscape; SC Consult—Sérgio Costa, construction manager
General contractor: Gaia Construtora—Renato Luis Gonçalves, Eduardo Busin
Structural system: reinforced concrete
Major materials: concrete, wood, glass, aluminium, limestone
Site area: 4,000 m²
Built area: 900 m²
Design: 2008
Construction: 2012

Deck on south 南側のテラス

Bathroom 浴室

SPBR ARQUITETOS
HOUSE IN RIBEIRÃO PRETO
Ribeirão Preto, São Paulo, Brazil
Photos: Yoshio Futagawa

The site for this single-family house originally sloped but has since been leveled and reconfigured to form a series of open boxes cut into ground. These regular wells accommodate four columns that carry the apparently weightless concrete container that is the house. Horizontal slabs of concrete, which define the interior upper and lower extremities of the courtyard-style house, are supported by up-stand beams located on top of the house. This carefully engineered design allows the interior spaces to remain free of columns while ensuring that the entire structure is effectively braced. Great sheets of glazing encase the living area at the front of the house, so that the eye can follow the framework from exterior to interior and puzzle the physics of the construction. Private and public areas are distinct by the U-shaped plan, while the kitchen does the connection between these two aspects of family life.

View from street on south 南側道路より見る

spbr arquitetos / House in Ribeirão Preto

Upper floor

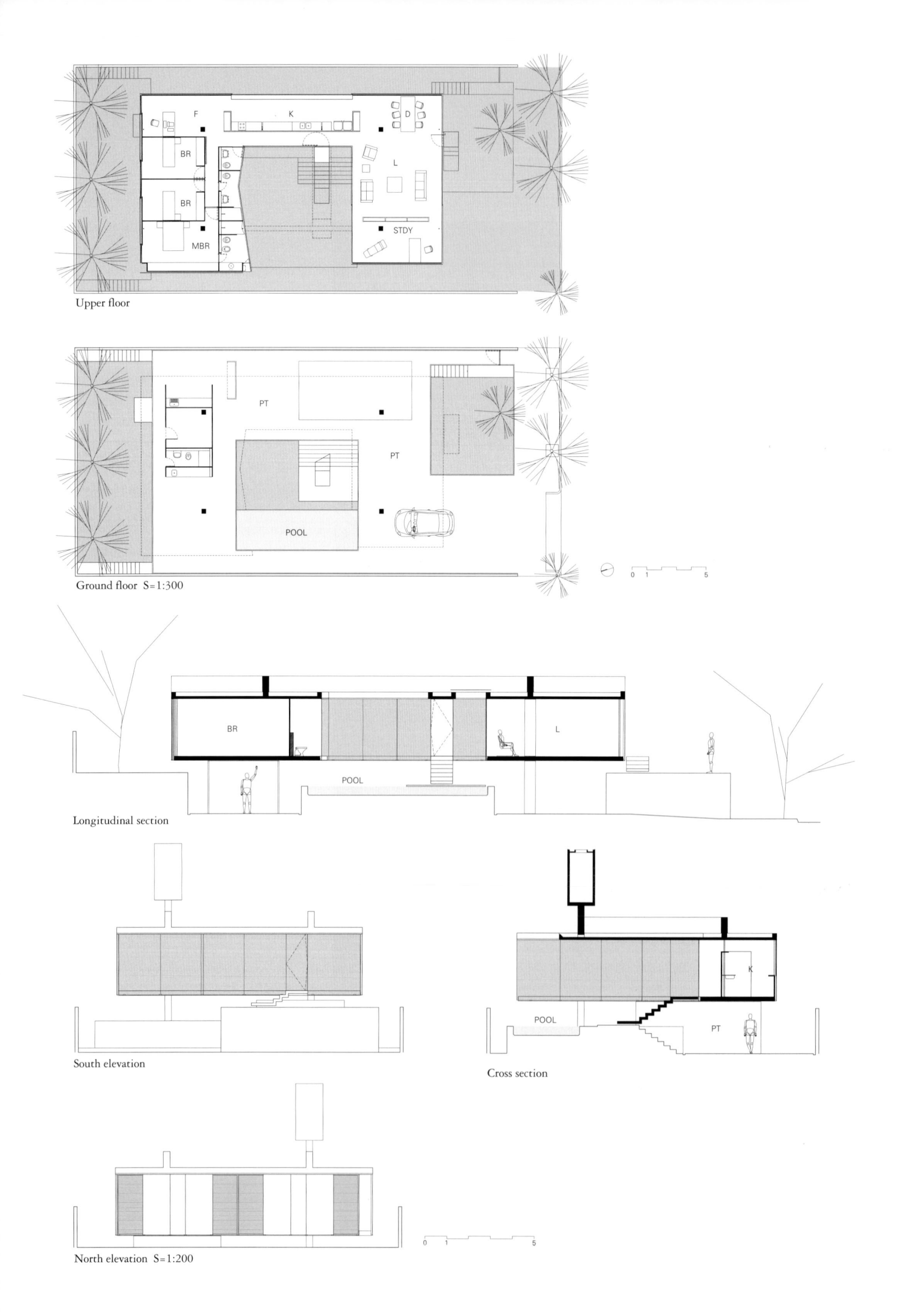

Ground floor S=1:300

Longitudinal section

South elevation

Cross section

North elevation S=1:200

Patio: looking north　パティオ：北を見る

Patio: looking south　パティオ：南を見る

spbr arquitetos / House in Ribeirão Preto 65

Stairs to swimming pool　プールへの階段

Swimming pool surrounded by two wings, water tank above　2つの棟に囲まれたプール。上に貯水槽

spbr arquitetos / House in Ribeirão Preto

Swimming pool　プール

　この家族の住宅の敷地は本来斜面地であった。敷地は開放的な箱を連続して地表面へと埋め込むために，平坦に造成されたものである。整然としたこれらの光の差し込む箱には4本の柱が立ち，非常に軽快に住宅のコンクリートのコンテナを支えている。水平スラブが上部の内部空間と中庭型の住宅の脚部を規定する。これらは住宅の頂部に配置された垂直梁によって支持されている。緻密に計画が行われた結果，内部には柱のない自由な空間が生まれ，構造全体ではブレースが効果的に機能するようになった。住宅正面のリビングは巨大なガラスによって覆われている。視線は構造の物理法則からは自由に，外部から内部へとフレームに沿って移る。プライベートとパブリックはU字型の平面計画によって区切られている。また，キッチンがこれらの異なる日常生活を結びつける役割を果たす。

Patio: view toward living room パティオ：居間方向を見る

Architects: spbr arquitetos—
Angelo Bucci, principal-in-charge;
Fernando de Mello Franco, Marta Moreira,
Milton Braga, architects; Anna Vilella,
Eduardo Ferroni, Maju Herklotz, Eliana Mello,
design team
Consultants: Jlbsen Puleo Uvo, structural;
Paulo Balugoli, construction
Program: private residence
Structural system: reinforced concrete
Major materials: concrete, glass
Site area: 450 m^2
Built area: 170 m^2
Design: 2000
Construction: 2001

spbr arquitetos / House in Ribeirão Preto

Dining/living room 居間／食堂

Living room 居間

Study on right　右に書斎

Kitchen　台所

spbr arquitetos / House in Ribeirão Preto

Upper floor. View of living/dining room from south garden 上階。南の庭より居間／食堂を見る

spbr arquitetos / House in Ribeirão Preto

SPBR ARQUITETOS
HOUSE AND STUDIO IN ORLANDIA
Orlandia, São Paulo, Brazil

Photos: Yoshio Futagawa

View from street on south 南側道路より見る

Architect: spbr arquitetos—
Angelo Bucci, principal-in-charge;
João Paulo Meirelles de Faria, Juliana Braga,
Tatiana Ozzetti, Nilton Suenaga,
Victor Próspero, Fernanda Cavallaro,
Lucas Nobre, project team
Consultant: Ibsen Puleo Uvo, structural;
Ricardo Heder, lighting; Raul Pereira, landscape; Paulo Balugoli, construction
Structural system: concrete
Major materials: concrete, wood, glass
Site area: 290.95 m^2
Built area: 382.87 m^2
Design: 2007-08
Construction: 2009-12

spbr arquitetos / House and Studio in Orlandia

Garage: salon on right　ガレージ：右はサロン

Garage: entrance on left　ガレージ：左は玄関

Entrance of salon　サロンの玄関

View from entrance. Access ramp to residence on right　玄関より見る。右は住宅に至る斜路

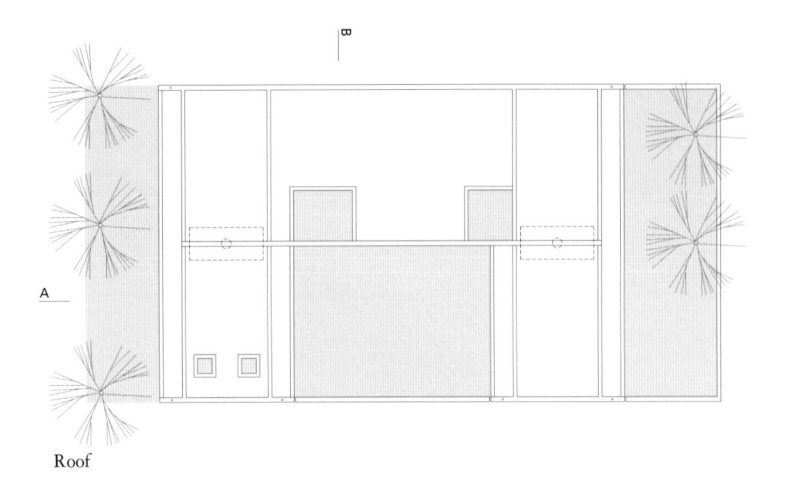

Roof

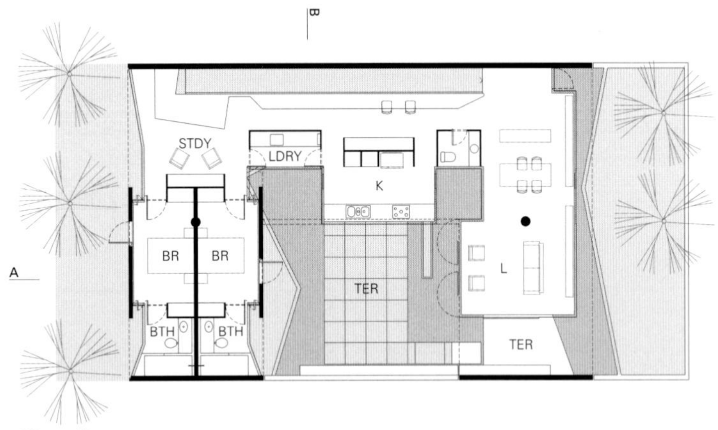

Upper floor

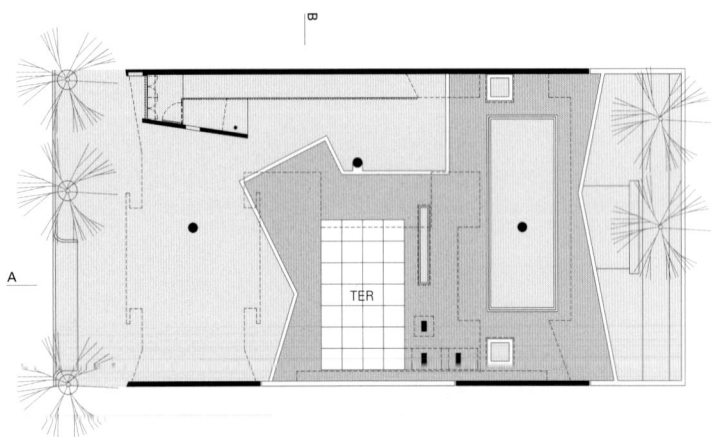

Intermediate level: terrace with water court

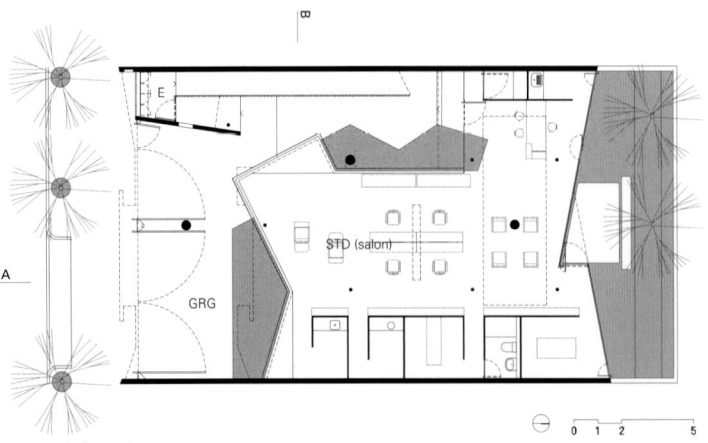

Ground floor S=1:300

A PROPER BALANCE AS A GOAL

Two activities: live and work. Its two corresponding spaces, house and studio, have been shaped historically, as two quite clear architectonic typologies.

Our first goal to this project was to combine both in a single small building, firstly keeping their programmatic independence and secondly achieving a proper balance in the whole (not a house with a studio appended, neither a studio with an added house).

It means, we would like to integrate both programs in such a way that both could live together with no conflicts. The studio should not be disturbed when the house is empty. In the same way, the house should not be degraded by an uninhabited studio.

STUDIO

The studio was disposed 1 meter lower the street level as a strategy to change the typical perception of a full-story building, then its function does not dominate the building.

Moreover, it is turned to the site's rear. In particular, a transparent facade enables the studio to benefit from a small garden conceived there.

In between the studio and the house there is an empty space that clarifies the in-

South elevation

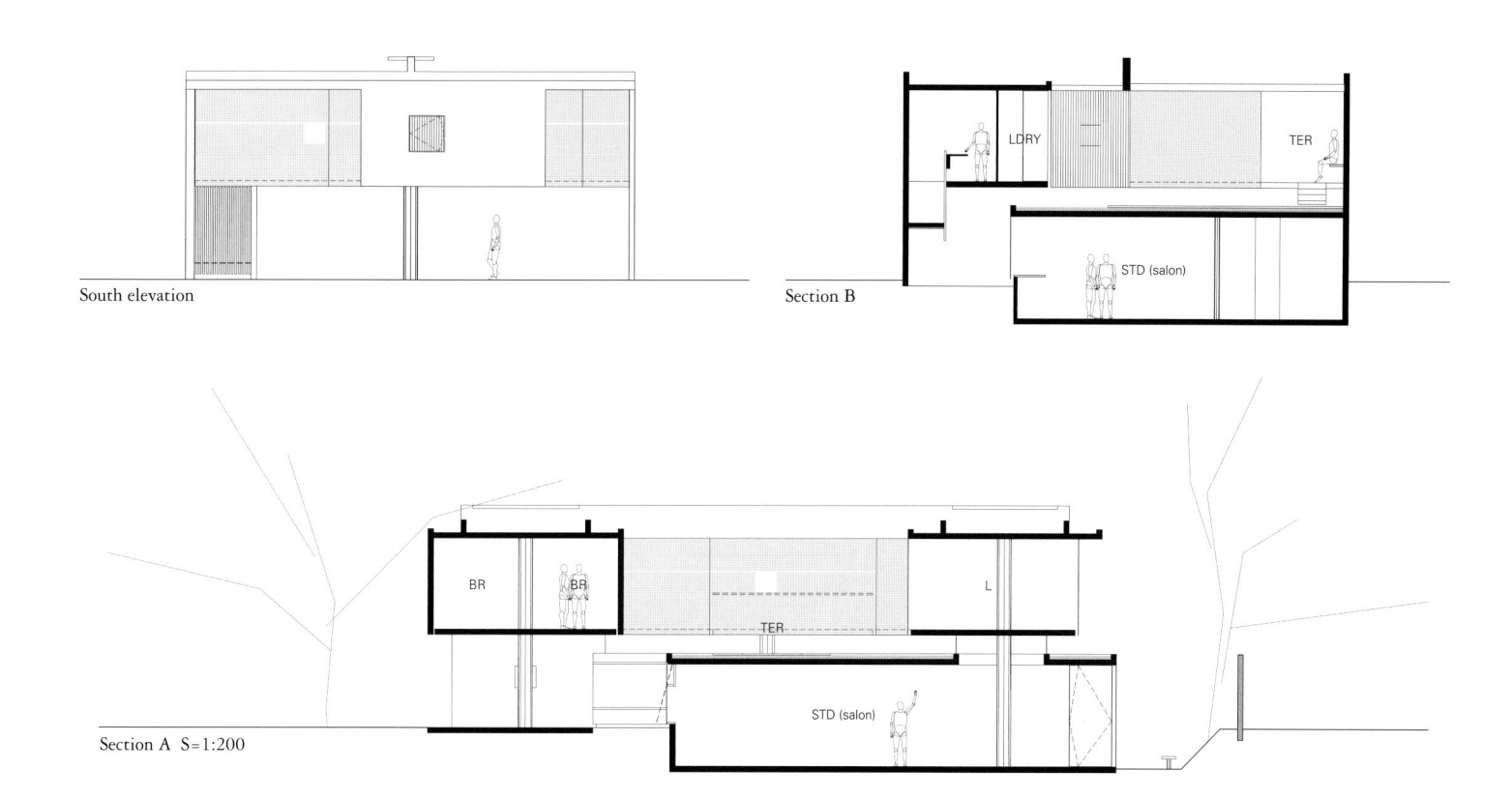

Section B

Section A S=1:200

dependence of the two programs.

HOUSE

At the west plot limit, the house entrance leads to a single-floor house, spread in the second level slab. The bedrooms are situated at the front side and the living room towards the rear. Connecting bedrooms and the living-room are the kitchen and service areas.

This program arrangement creates an inner court making an opportune use of the studio's roof slab as a reflecting pool.

The reflecting pool mitigates the severe local weather and multiplies the light in the house patio. In addition, it assures the impermeability of the concrete slab, free of any membrane, and works as thermal insulation for the studio.

The house's design aimed for no evident architectonic elements like doors and windows. Thus, its function is not apprehended at first glance in order to not prevail over the studio.

TWO MAJOR CONSTRUCTION MATERIALS

Both programs are being built with few major materials: glass and concrete.

This conciseness is a strategy to keep construction process and costs under control.

〈バランスの取れた空間〉

二つの活動：生活と仕事。住宅とスタジオはこれらの機能を満たす空間として，それぞれ歴史的に非常に明快な建築的タイポロジーを形成してきた。

この計画の第一の目標は，両者を単一の小規模建築へと結びつけることである。そのためにはプログラムの独立性を維持し，次いで（スタジオを付随した住宅，あるいは住宅付きのスタジオといったものとは異なる）全体の調和を適切に保つことが求められた。

そのため，両者が矛盾することなく共存するプログラムの統合が検討された。住宅に人が不在の際にスタジオの利用が妨げられず，また，逆の場合でも住宅の環境が悪化しないようにする必要があった。

〈スタジオ〉

スタジオは道路レベルから1メートル低く配置されている。これは2階建ての建築の常識を覆すための方法である。この建築では単一の機能が全体を支配することがない。

また，スタジオは敷地の背後に計画された。スタジオからはとりわけ透明なファサードを通し，裏庭に計画された小さな庭園を楽しむことができる。

スタジオと住宅のあいだには空白を挿入することで，これらの二つのプログラムは独立性が明確に区別されるようになった。

〈住宅〉

住宅のエントランスは西側の敷地境界線沿いにある。上階の平屋の住宅にはここから入ることができる。寝室は前面に位置し，一方，リビングは背面に向けられている。寝室とリビングを結びつけているのはキッチンとサービス空間である。

スタジオの屋根をリフレクティング・プールとして利用する中庭がつくられたのは，このプログラム構成によるところである。リフレクティング・プールは厳しい気候を和らげるとともに，住宅のパティオに光を引き込む役割を果たす。また，コンクリートスラブへの雨水の浸透を確実に防ぎ，塗膜防水を施すことなくスタジオの断熱層として機能する。

この住宅には扉や窓といった明快な建築的要素は存在しない。そのため住宅の持つ機能は一見，不明瞭で，スタジオに対して優位にあるわけではない。

〈二つの主要な構造素材〉

双方のプログラムはガラスとコンクリートの限られた素材で構成される。

建設工程と予算を管理するため，このように簡潔な構造が採用された。

Salon: view toward reception　サロン：受付方向を見る

Salon　サロン

Window: wooden handle on right to open
窓：右の木製ハンドルで開閉する

Salon: garden on north サロン：北側の庭

Ramp to upper floor (residence) 上階（住居棟）へ至る斜路

Study 書斎

Living room: looking south 居間：南を見る

Dining table designed by architect 建築家によるデザインの食卓

spbr arquitetos / House and Studio in Orlandia

Terrace テラス

Living room 居間

Kitchen 台所

Opening of kitchen 台所の開口部

Bedroom 寝室

View toward bedroom from study 書斎より寝室を見る

Terrace: kitchen on left　テラス：左は台所

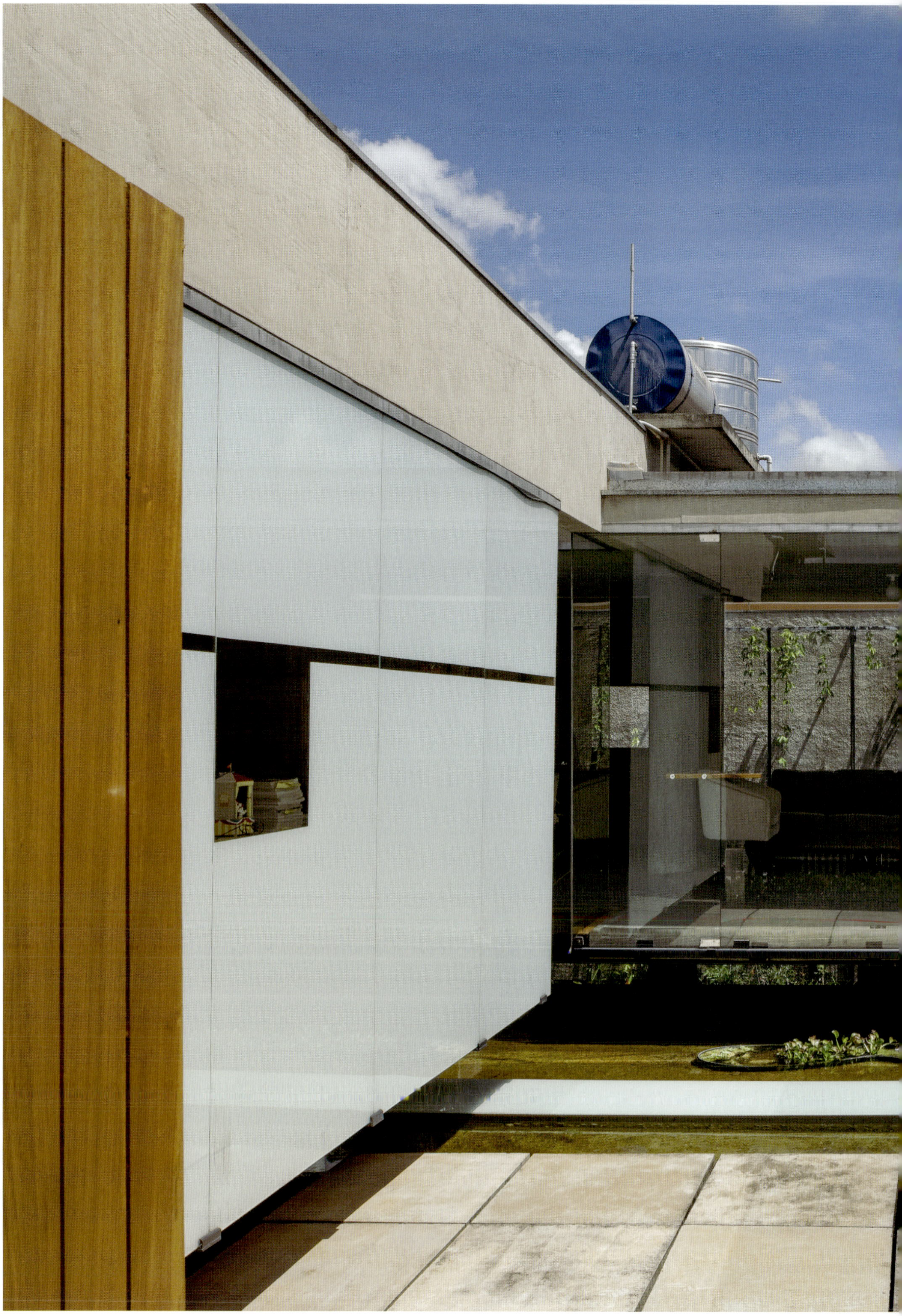

Terrace with water court 水庭とテラス

HIRONAKA OGAWA
BELLOWS HOUSE
Takamatsu, Kagawa, Japan
Photos: Yoshio Futagawa

Overall view from southeast 南東より見る全景

Siteplan S=1:800

East elevation

Loft

West elevation

Second floor

South elevation

First floor S=1:200

North elevation S=1:200

Hironaka Ogawa / Bellows House 91

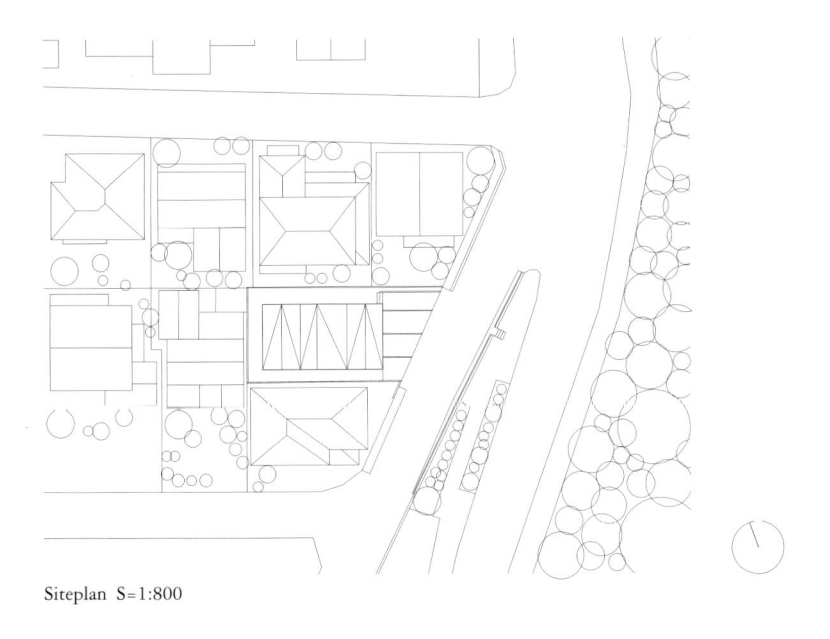

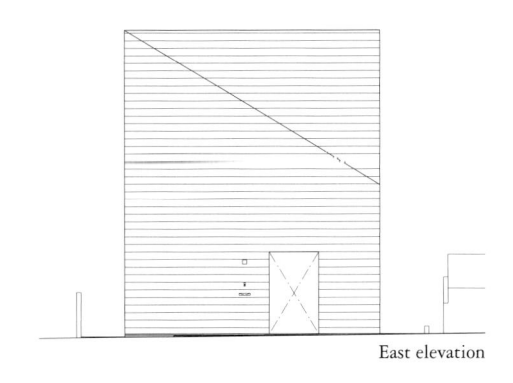

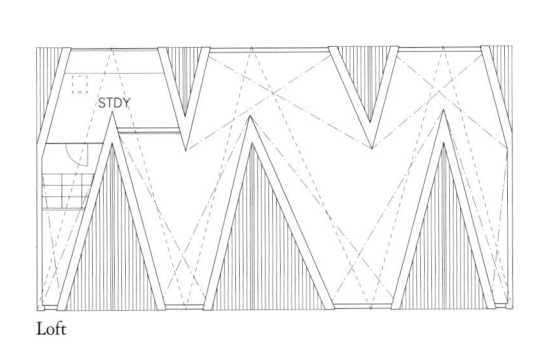

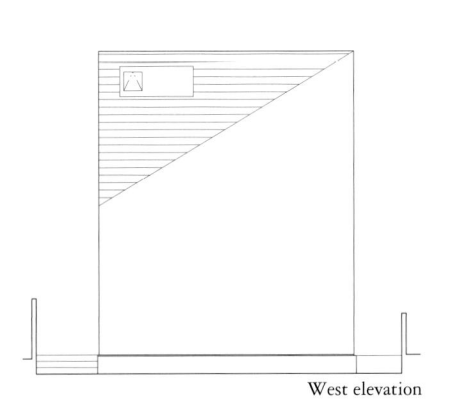

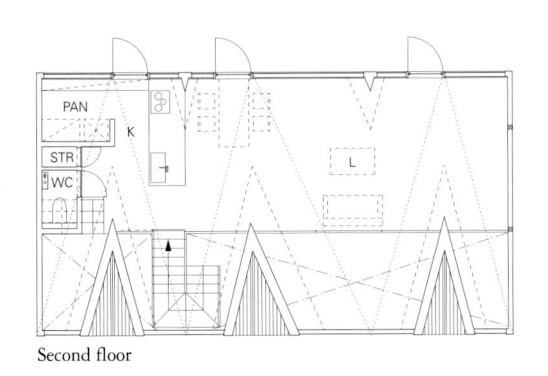

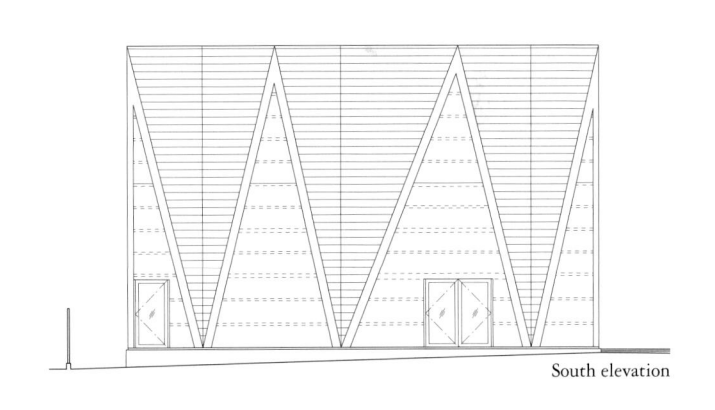

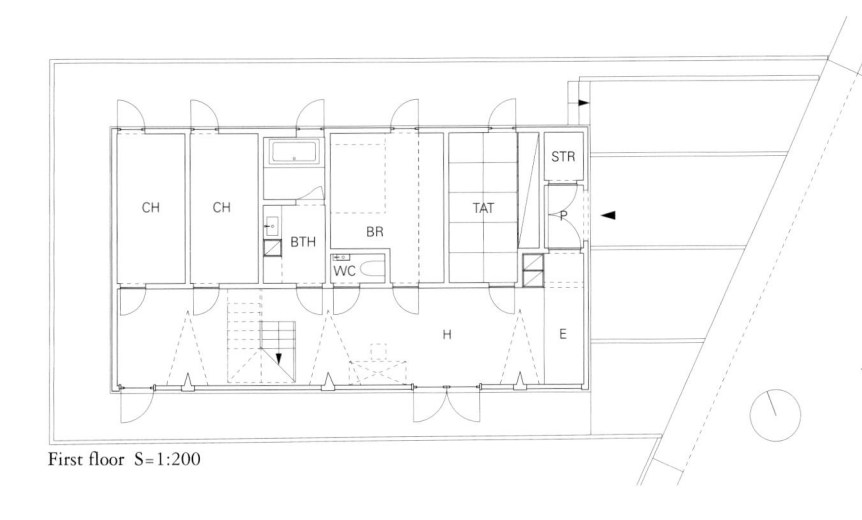

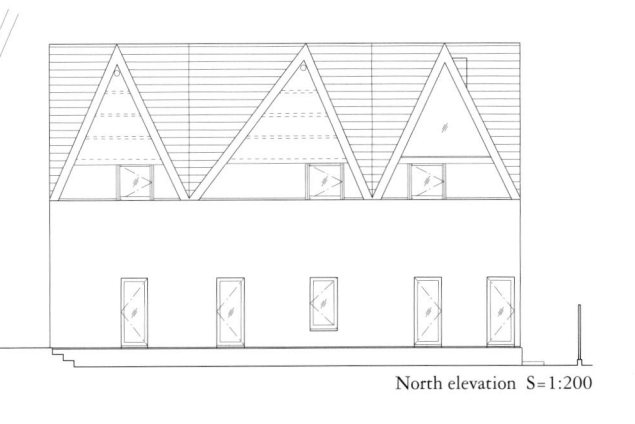

View from northeast 北東より見る

The residence is built in Takamatsu city for a married couple, two children and a cat. Since three sides are surrounded by neighboring houses and the client did not request a yard, the interior space was elaborated.

The hall at the entrance is public space for piano classes and is connected to the living room on the second floor through a void. In addition to a study on a loft, each individual room to secure privacy between the family members was placed on the first floor. A living room/dining room/kitchen, which serves as family's public space, was positioned on the second floor.

Looking just at the plans, it may feel very simple and less varied. However, an inward-tucked roof covering the public space plays a role as a wall, giving territories to the one room spaces such as the hall and the living room/dining room/kitchen. At the same time, it gently connects each space. Moreover, folded roof's triangle gable sides, which are made by sandwiching translucent insulation with waving polycarbonate boards, enable bright lighting and also erase the presence of forthcoming neighboring houses on the three sides of the site. As a result, ample light is brought to the neighboring land through some valleys of the folded roof on the outer space and a comfortable relationship with the neighboring houses is made even without a yard.

The space gains elasticity like bellows by the folded roof. Indeed, folding the space creates a strange sense of deepness. Furthermore, an addition of various sections produces more contented and diverse space.
Hironaka Ogawa

Entrance hall on first floor　1階，玄関ホール

View toward entrance from staircase 階段室より玄関方向を見る

Upward view of staircase 階段室の見上げ

高松市内に建つ，夫婦と子供2人，猫1匹のための住宅。三方を隣家に囲まれており，庭はいらないという施主の要望により，内部空間の充実を図った。

玄関を入ってからのホールはピアノ教室のためのパブリックスペースとなっており，吹き抜けを介して2階のリビングと繋がっている。また，ロフトの書斎以外に1階に家族間のプライバシーを確保するための各個室を用意し，家族のパブリックスペースとなるリビング・ダイニング・キッチンは2階に配置している。

プランだけを見ると非常にシンプルで変化のないものに感じるかもしれないが，パブリックスペースにおいて，内部へ折り込まれた屋根を被せることでそれらが壁的な役割も果たし，ホールやリビング・ダイニング・キッチンのワンルーム空間にテリトリーを与えつつ各スペースを緩やかに繋いでいる。また，この折り込まれた屋根によってできた三角形の妻側面は，透光性のある断熱材をポリカーボネイトの波板でサンドイッチした壁面として，敷地三面に迫る隣家の存在を消しながらも明るい採光を確保している。結果，外部においても，幾つかの折り込まれた屋根の谷間によって隣地にも十分な光が差し込み，庭がなくてもゆとりのある関係を隣家と築いている。

折り込まれた屋根によって空間はジャバラのような伸縮性を獲得し，まさに空間が折られることによって不思議な奥行き感が生まれ，さらに，そこに断面の変化も加わることで，より豊かで多様な空間となっている。 (小川博央)

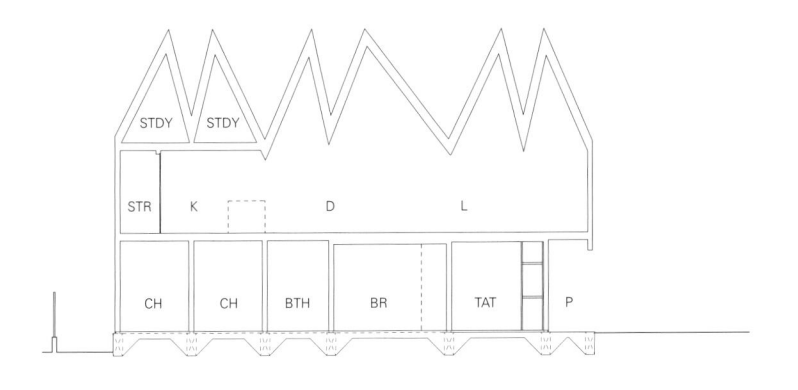

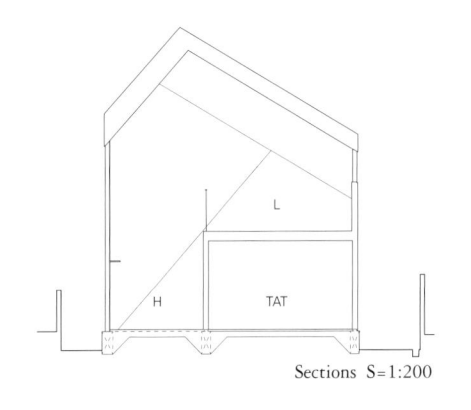

Sections S=1:200

Hironaka Ogawa / Bellows House

Axonometric

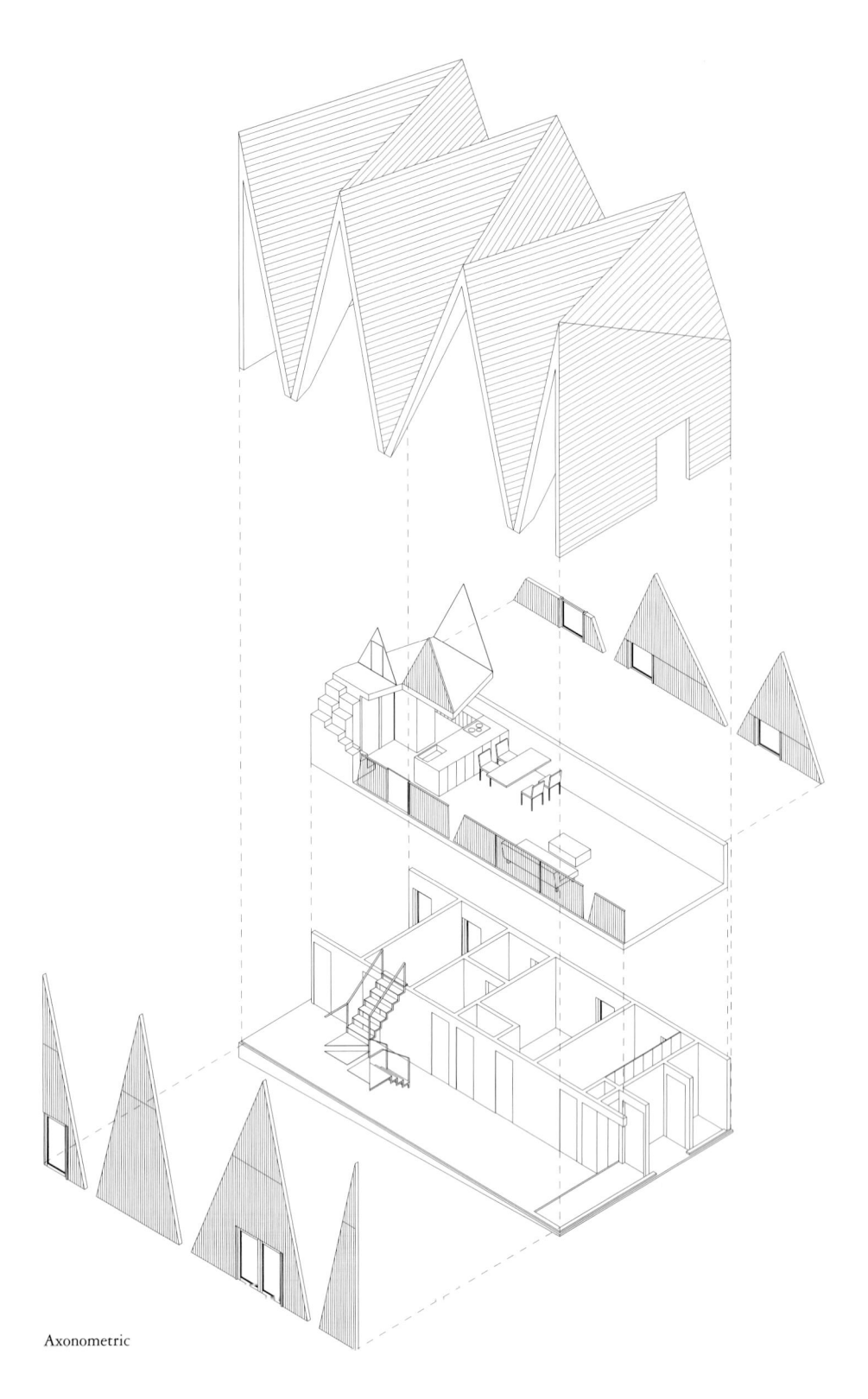

Dining room and kitchen on second floor 2階，食堂と台所

Architects: Hironaka Ogawa & Associates—
Hironaka Ogawa, principal-in-charge;
Akihiro Furukawa, project team
Consultants: Takashi Manda Structural
Design—Takashi Manda, structural
General contractor: Uehara Construction Co.,
Ltd.—Takeru Morimoto
Structural system: timber frame
Major materials: galvanized steel, metal
siding, corrugated polycarbonate sheets,
exterior; vinyl cloth, vinyl tile flooring, interior
Site area: 187.11 m^2
Built area: 87.04 m^2
Total floor area: 143.32 m^2
Design: 2011-13
Construction: 2013

Living room with void above hall 居間とホールの吹抜け

Kitchen 台所

Living room: view toward void　居間：吹抜け方向を見る

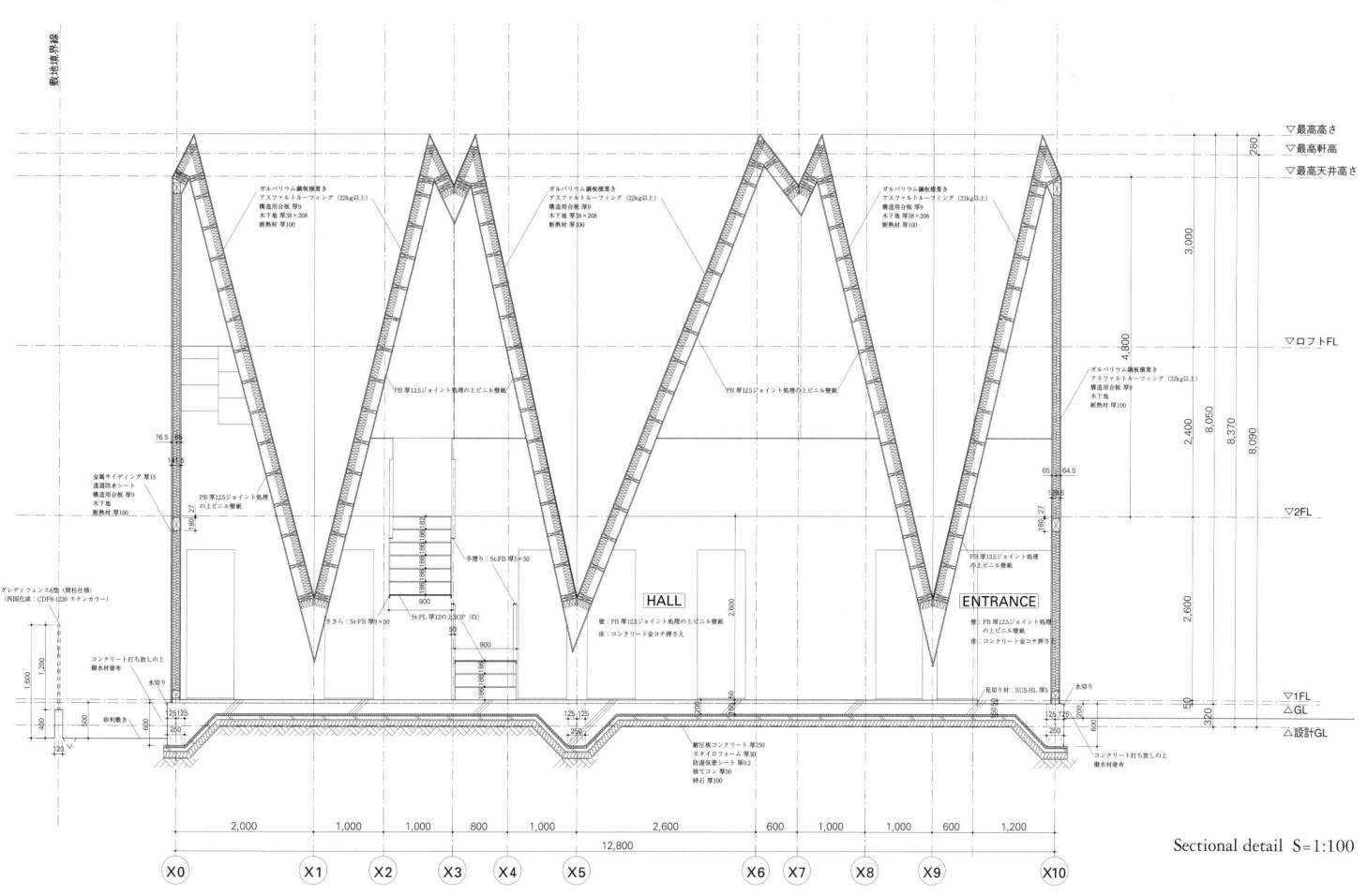

Sectional detail S=1:100

Hironaka Ogawa / Bellows House

RYO ABE
PERFIL
Tokyo, Japan

Photos: Katsumasa Tanaka

Evening view from south 南より見る夕景

At the corner of this centrally located, old residential area, where mansions with gardens once used to stand, it is difficult to find continuity among the streets of bristling small homes that cover the now subdivided land. Yet inside each of these houses, one can discover common elements that reflect the life that is being led there. A pilotis parking that occupies most of the above-ground floors, a nominal entrance, modest greens planted near site boundaries, windows and verandas as accents for the facade, house-shapes without roof trusses, etc. Restructuring these elements will create a house that is similar to the profile of this street corner. I wanted to create an environment where scenes of life are generated both within and without this profile (perfil).

Eight steel pillars are driven into the underground supporting foundation, with raft-shaped steel beams that are joined over the pillars to build a steel framework. Like a tree growing from the ground, a steel plate structured core was positioned at the center of the house, where functionalities like storage and bedrooms are layered to simultaneously achieve lifestyle foundations and architectural strength. The raw steel, which changes slowly over time, is treated as something that exists close to the physical bodies of the residents. Other interior finishes are constructed using natural materials too such as wooden boards and stucco, with "rough" and "uneven" characteristics

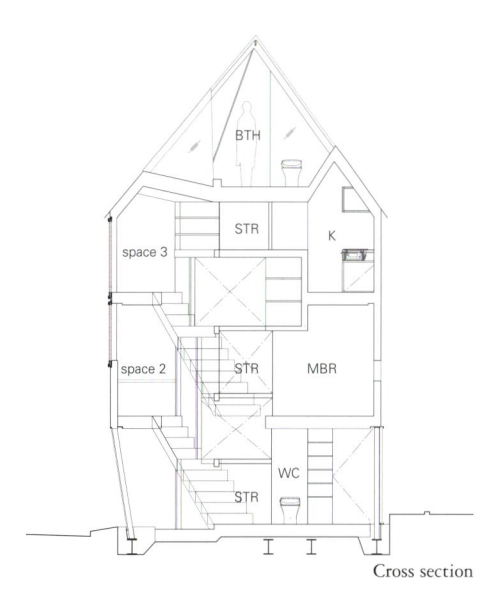

Cross section

which create a spatial texture that speaks to the resident's sensibility. The sanitary area at the core top creates an indoors view with numerous house-shaped ceilings. Furthermore, the outer shell is punctured with a large house-shaped opening towards the city, creating an area with ambiguous interior/exterior consciousness. The spatial experience of this area is even more amplified by the approach, which has been positioned with enough room from the north-side boundary, and by pushing the entire house closer towards the east and south street boundaries. Aspects of the city overlays the scenes of life indoors, and the life spent inside are exposed as part of the city. Direct and indirect lighting from the openings and the top-side light affect the spatial texture by the hour. The house is designed as a profile (perfil) that provokes the sensibilities of city life—where conversations between the house and the residents are born in moments when the "heart" senses the phenomenon caught in this area, faster than the "mind" is able to process it.

Unifying experiences of life and the city are created around each house, which gradually integrate to replace the streets with new and organic sceneries. My aim is to create the city's "profile (perfil)" that becomes the origination of this change.

Ryo Abe

South elevation S=1:150

Evening view of first floor 1階夕景

Staircase on first floor　1階階段室

View from entrance toward south　玄関より南を見る

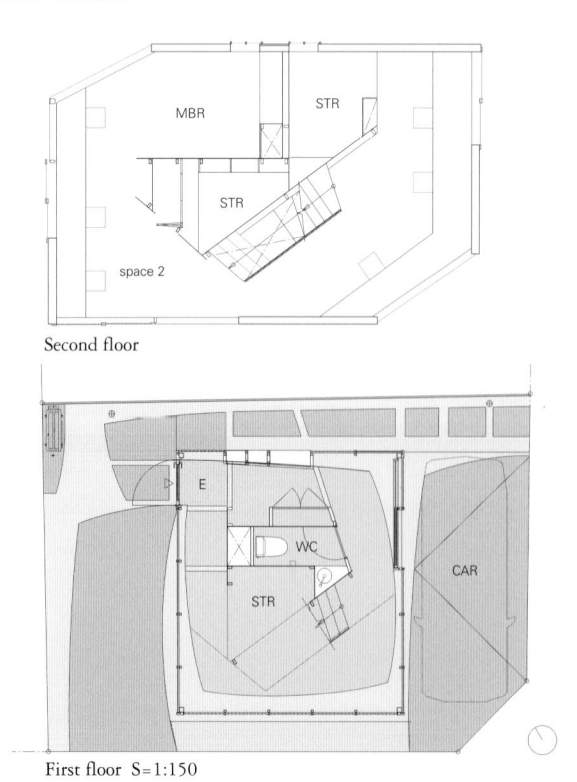

Second floor

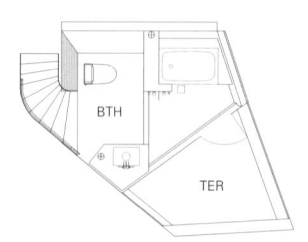

Third floor (GL+6,500)

First floor　S=1:150

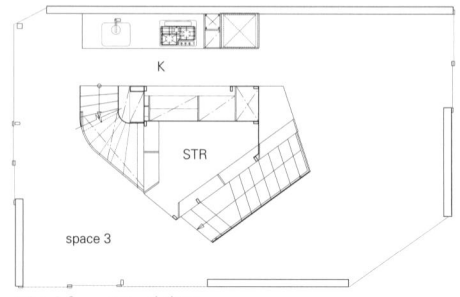

Third floor (GL+4,400)

Sectional details S=1:15

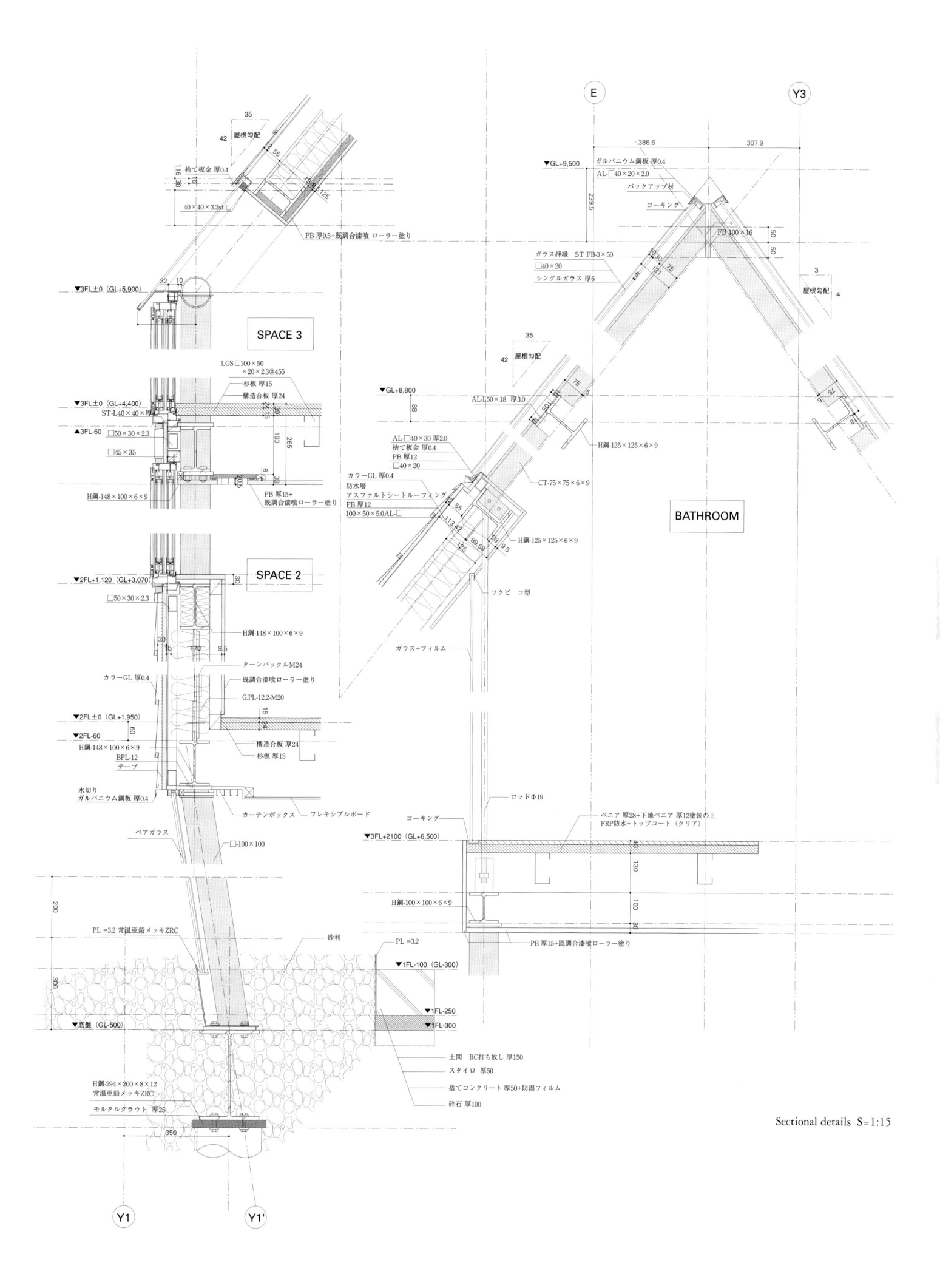

Space 2 on second floor　2階スペース2

Storage on second floor　2階収納

Space 2: looking storage　スペース２：収納を見る

Storage　収納

Space 2　スペース２

かつて庭付きの屋敷がたっていた都心の古い住宅街，敷地が分譲されて極小住宅が林立するこの一角では，町並みとよべる連続性を見つけることは難しいが，それぞれの住宅の中にここでの生活像を反映した様々な共通要因を発見することができる。地上階を占拠するピロティ駐車場と申しわけ程度の玄関，隣地境界のささやかな植栽，外観アクセントとしての窓やベランダ，小屋組のない家型，etc。それらの要素を再構築すれば，この街かどの輪郭のような建築がつくれるだろう。その輪郭の内外に生活の風景が発生する環境をつくり出したいと考えた。

地中の支持地盤まで8本の鉄骨杭を打ち込み，その上に筏状の鉄骨梁を接合し，鉄骨造の架構を立ち上げる。地中から生える樹木をイメージしながら住宅の中心に収納や寝室や生活機能を重層させた鉄板構造のコアを配置し，生活の基盤と建築の強度を同時につくり出している。室内でゆっくりとした経年変化をする素地の鉄を生活者の肉体に近い存在として扱い，その他の内部仕上げも素地の木板，漆喰など，「粗さ」や「斑」をもった自然素材で構成し，生活者の感受性に働きかける「肌理」を空間につくり出している。コア最上部のサニタリー空間は室内に幾つもの家型天井が連なる風景をつくり出し，さらに外殻には街に対して大きな家型の開口が穿たれて，内外の意識が曖昧な領域をつくり出している。北側の隣地境界に対して余裕を持った配置でアプローチ空間をつくり，建築全体を東南の道路境界ギリギリまでせり出すことで，この領域の空間体験をより一層際立たせている。街の様相が室内の生活風景と重なり，内部の生活が街の要素として露出する，開口やトップサイドライトから差し込む直接光と間接光が空間の「肌理」を刻々と変化させる。領域に現れた現象を「脳」が理解するよりはやく「心」で感じた瞬間，生活者との間に会話が生まれる，街の中に生活する感受性を誘発させる輪郭として建築を設計している。

街と一体となった生活体験がそれぞれの建築の周囲につくり出され，それらが緩やかに繋がってゆく事で，町並みに代る，新しい，有機的な風景が育まれるだろう。その発端となる，まちの「輪郭」をつくることを目指している。

（安部良）

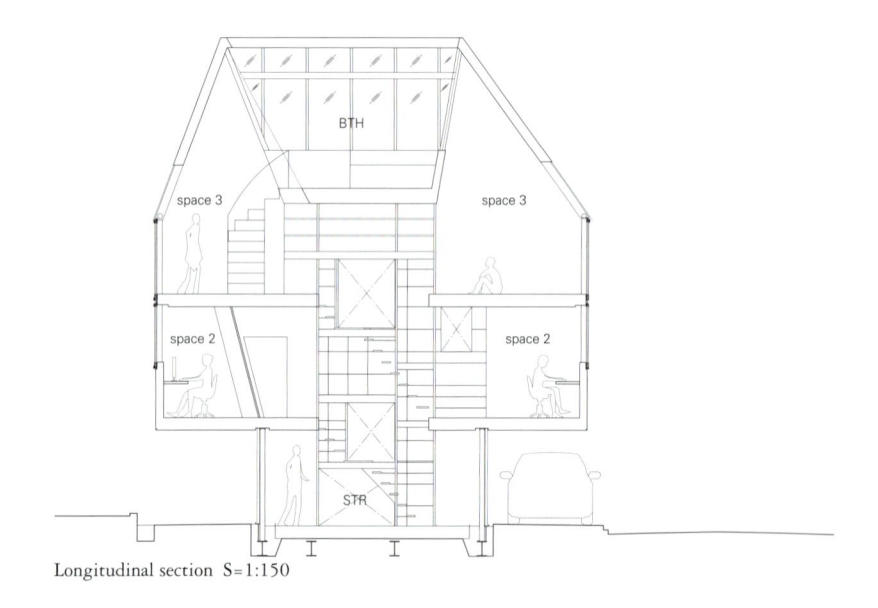

Longitudinal section S=1:150

Space 3 on third floor　3階スペース3

Space 3: kitchen on right　スペース 3：右が台所

Bathroom 浴室

Kitchen 台所

Architects: Architects Atelier Ryo Abe—
Ryo Abe, principal-in-charge;
Atsushi Osawa, Keiji Yorita, project team
Consultants: Mitsuhiro Kanada,
Kengo Takamatsu, structural;
Architects Atelier Ryo Abe, mechanical;
MAXRAY, lighting; CASTIE, bathtab
General contractor:
Yokomizo Construction Company
Structural system: steel
Major materials: steel sheet, pair glass, exterior; steel plate, plaster, mortar, plywood, ceder board, interior
Site area: 68.92 m²
Building area: 45.51 m²
Total floor area: 122.96 m²
Design: 2010-13
Construction: 2013-14

MARCOS ACAYABA
HELIO OLGA HOUSE
São Paulo, Brazil
Photos: Yoshio Futagawa

Overall view from studio on north　北側のスタジオより見る

Industrialized wooden structures allow me to build on very challenging terrains, and fully realize my ideal of lightness, a permanent challenge to gravity.

In addition to speeding up the construction work, and enabling it to be cleaner, timber structures minimize the impact on the natural environment.

This house was conceived as a prototype of industrialized housing for uneven sites. I designed Helio Olga House for an engineer and manufacturer of wooden structures.

In 1987 I had just started to design industrialized wooden structures.

There were three houses under construction, all of them being produced by Helio Olga in his factory. Then he asked me to design his own house.

In terms of orientation I had a problem: if the house were built parallel to the street, simpler to reach the ground, I would have little sunlight in the winter and excess in the summer. In addition, a construction across the street makes shadow from the northwest. (1)

So I found that the best position for the house was perpendicular to the street. This presented a challenge: the height of the structure! Then I thought of a bridge structure. (2)

Considering the required room dimensions, and the height of the ceiling, I adopted a structural cubic module of 3.3 meters with 10 m² each. After some sketches I reached the final solution (3), an equation which considers:
- The Functional Spaces: 10 modules for living and kitchen, 6 modules for family bedrooms, 2 for guestroom, and 2 for a playroom,
- The Structural Balance: symmetric,
- The Assembling System: without scaffolding or props, growing upwards symmetrically. (4)

The whole structure was assembled by three workers in 45 days, with no need for scaffolding or further equipment. The waste material was reduced to a minimum, and the final cost was half the one in current buildings, in such uneven sites, in Brazil.

6 concrete columns sunk 10 meters into the soil, emerge above ground, leaving its original profile intact. They support three symmetrical structural bays, consisting of a framework of pillars, beams and sties. Columns and beams are connected at the nodes by steel bolts, to which the sties are anchored. The transversal sties absorb stresses from the wind, and also transfer the weight from the central columns to the side bays.

All the components of this structure play a precise and evident static role. The main wooden structure absorbs flexo-compression stresses. The metal connections and the sties absorb the tensile stresses. And the concrete columns the weight of the entire construction. I always avoid material that is not essential, selecting it for its specific performance and structural qualities. All the materials must work together in a way that fully expresses their properties.

On the top level, with garage and swimming pool in concrete, there is a further point of contact between the timber structure and the ground in order to resist lateral winds through vertical steel bolts, transmitting just horizontal efforts. The timber structure is simetric and balanced, and doesn't allow further accidental vertical efforts.

The structure is filled by indstrialized white plywood pannels, and wood shutters.

The main spaces were organized in an "L" shaped upper floor: garage and pool on a concrete structure, directly on the ground, and service area, kitchen, dining and living room on the wooden structure. The pool terrace is close to the garage. If you park the cars on the street, and if you open some sliding glass doors, you transform the garage into a covered space for parties, for example.

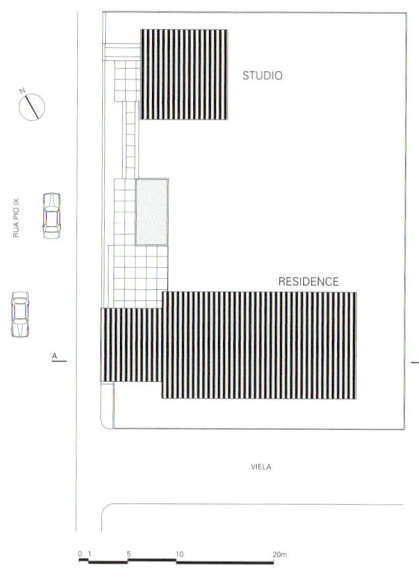

Site plan S=1:750

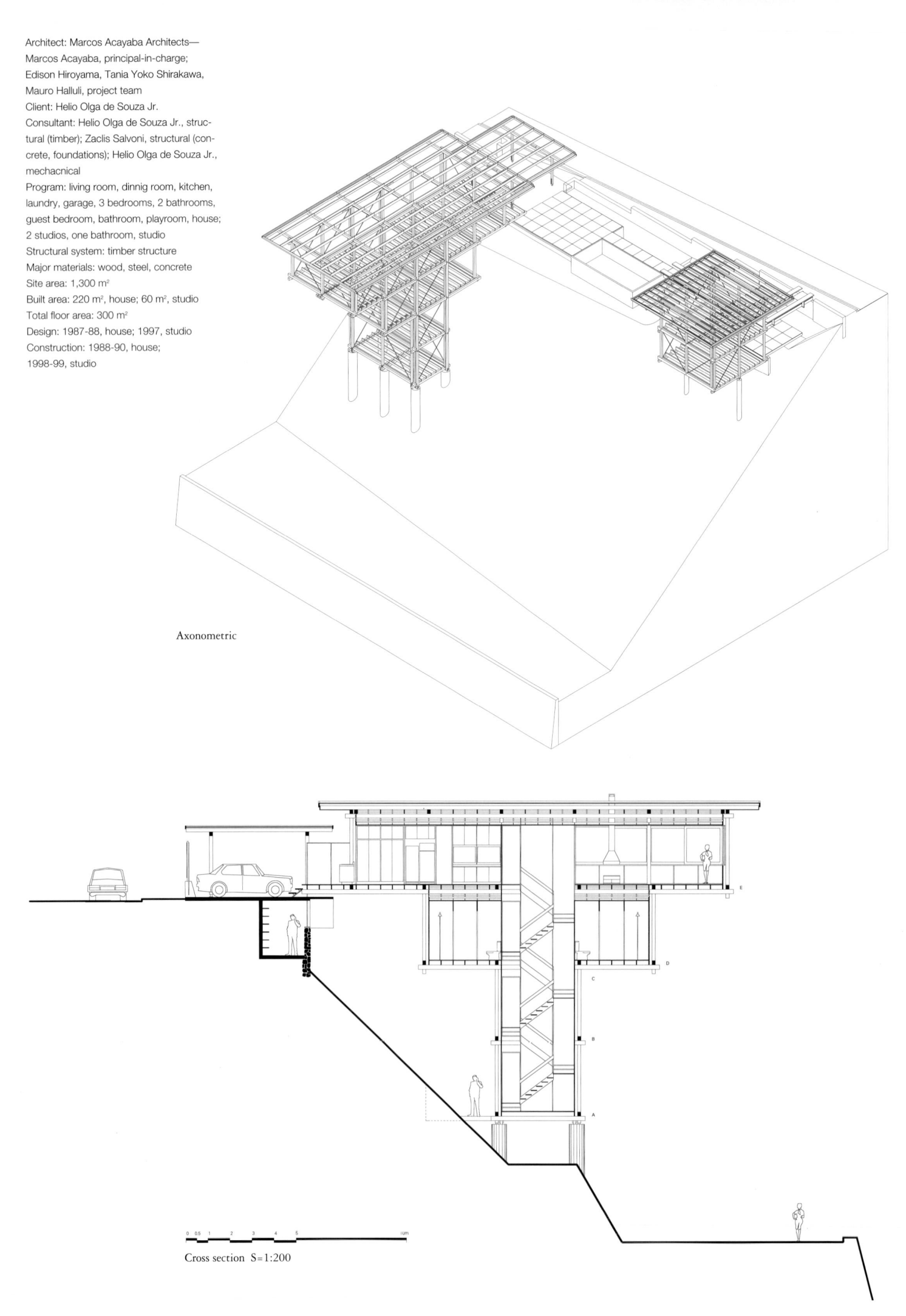

Architect: Marcos Acayaba Architects—
Marcos Acayaba, principal-in-charge;
Edison Hiroyama, Tania Yoko Shirakawa,
Mauro Halluli, project team
Client: Helio Olga de Souza Jr.
Consultant: Helio Olga de Souza Jr., structural (timber); Zaclis Salvoni, structural (concrete, foundations); Helio Olga de Souza Jr., mechacnical
Program: living room, dinnig room, kitchen, laundry, garage, 3 bedrooms, 2 bathrooms, guest bedroom, bathroom, playroom, house; 2 studios, one bathroom, studio
Structural system: timber structure
Major materials: wood, steel, concrete
Site area: 1,300 m²
Built area: 220 m², house; 60 m², studio
Total floor area: 300 m²
Design: 1987-88, house; 1997, studio
Construction: 1988-90, house; 1998-99, studio

Axonometric

Cross section S=1:200

View from north: wooden bridge structure　北より見る：木造ブリッジ状構造

Upward view of southeast elevation　南東面見上げ

Detail of concrete column and wooden structure
コンクリートの柱と木構造の取り合い

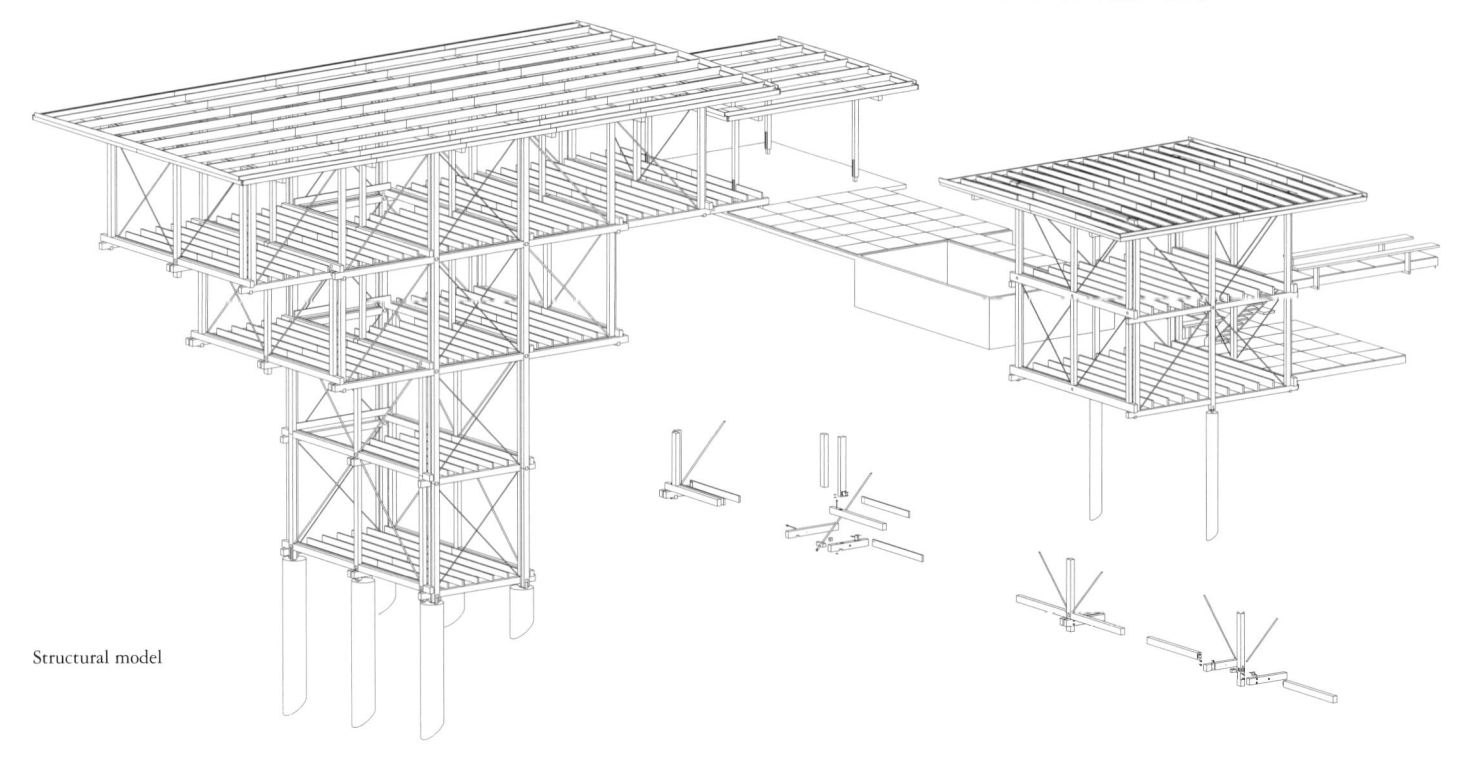

Structural model

114

Upper level S=1:200

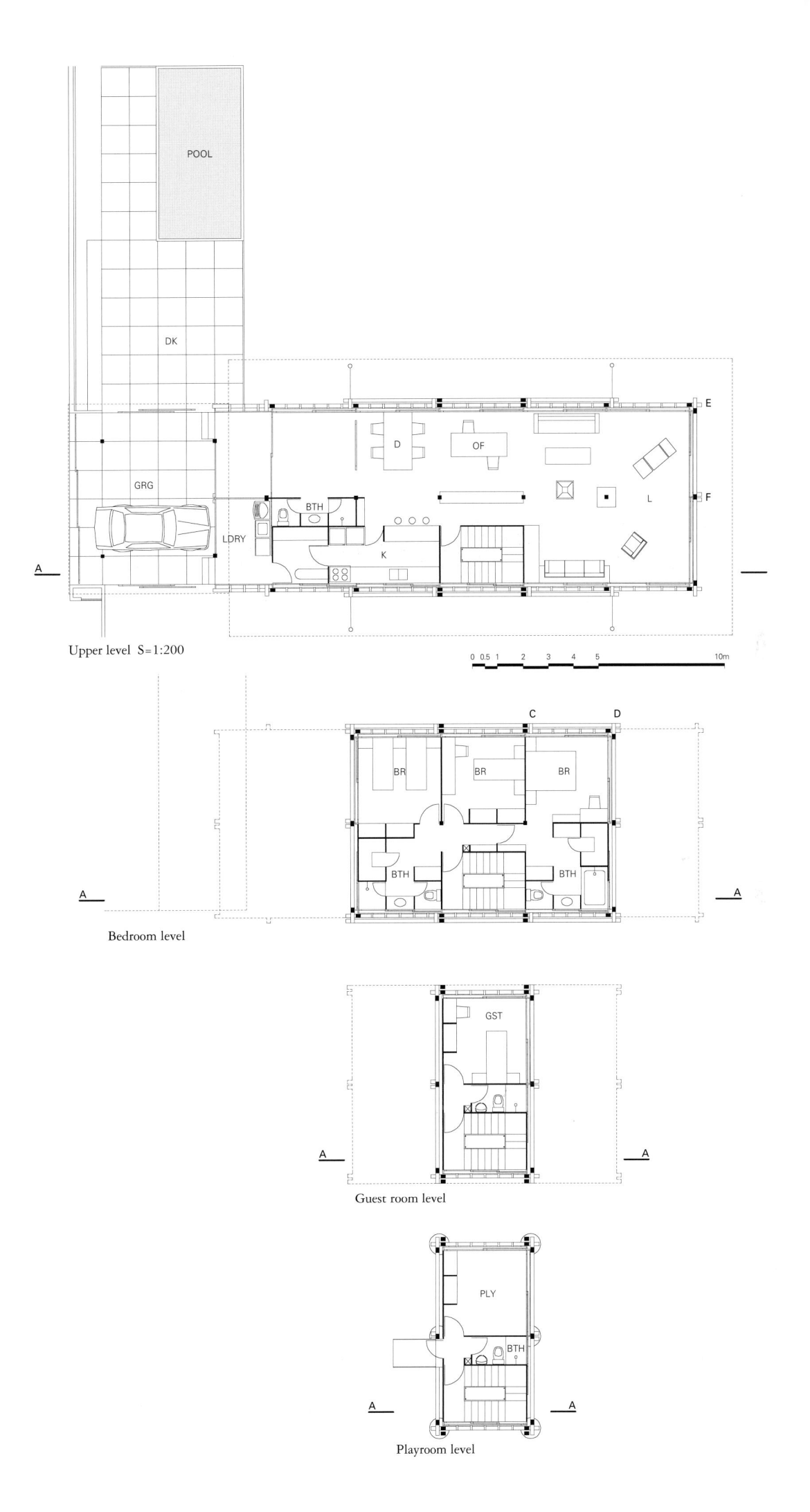

0 0.5 1 2 3 4 5 10m

Bedroom level

Guest room level

Playroom level

Marcos Acayaba / Helio Olga House 115

View from pool on north　北側のプールより見る

View from pool toward studio　プールよりスタジオを見る

　木構造が工業化されたことで非常に挑戦的な形を実現できるようになり，重力への絶え間ない挑戦とも言える軽さの理想を現実化させることもできた。木構造は施工のスピードが速くより綺麗に仕上げられることに加えて，自然環境へのインパクトを最小限に抑えることができる。
　この住宅は高低差のある敷地に建つ工業化住宅のプロトタイプとして考えられた。私はこのエリオ・オルガ・ハウスを木構造のエンジニアと製造業者のために設計したのである。
　1987年，私はまだ工業的な木構造をデザインし始めたばかりであった。当時は三つの家が工事中で，どれもエリオ・オルガの工場で生産されていた。そしてある時，彼は自邸を設計して

Upward view of studio　スタジオ見上げ

ほしいと私に依頼してきたのだ。

　家の配置の向きに関して，私は少々問題を抱えていた。道路に平行に家を置きシンプルに地面に設置させると，冬は十分な日射が得られず逆に夏は日射が多すぎてしまう。さらに通りを挟んで行われる施工作業によって北西の方から影ができてしまう。

　そのため，通りに対して垂直に家を置くのが最適な配置であると結論づけた。しかし同時にこれは挑戦的なことでもあった。構造体の高さの問題である。私はそこでブリッジ状の構造体を思いついた。

　要求された部屋の大きさと天井高を考慮して，構造体の四角いモジュールをそれぞれ3.3メートル角10平米の大きさに定めた。そして幾つかスケッチを繰り返した後，最終的な解決策に辿り着いた。その方程式は以下のような三つを考慮している。

・機能的な空間：リビングルームはモジュール10個分，家族の寝室は6個分，ゲストルームとプレイルームがそれぞれ2個ずつ
・構造的なバランス：左右対称
・施工システム：足場や支えを使うことなく，左右対称なまま上に建てていく

　構造体の組み立ては足場や特別な器具を用いることなく，わずか3人の作業者によって45日間でできてしまう。これにより廃棄される建材を最小限に抑えることができ，また最終的なコストは現在のブラジルにおけるこのような高低差のある敷地でのビル建設に比べて半分で済む。

　10メートルの深さまで打ち込まれた6本のコンクリート柱は地上にも顔を出し，その特性をそのまま見せている。これらが柱，梁，各部屋によるフレームワークで構成された左右対称な三層の構造体を支えている。柱と梁は接合部をスティールボルトで接合され各ボックスをしっかりと固定している。横に広がるような部屋の形は風による負荷を吸収し中央の柱にかかる重さを両翼へと受け流してくれる。

　この構造体の構成要素は全てが一体となり建物にしっかりとした安定性を生み出している。主構造である木の部材が圧縮荷重を負担し，金属のブレースと各ボックスが引張力を負担する。またコンクリートの柱は建物の重量を全て受け止める。

　私はそれが本質的ではないという理由から，常に構造的な質とある特定のパフォーマンスだけを求める素材選びを避けるようにしている。すべての素材は一体となって完璧にその能力を発揮できなければならないのだ。

　最上階のレベルでは構造体と斜面頂部が離れており，コンクリートの床のガレージとプールがこれを結んでいる。これにより横からの風を垂直の杭で受け水平応力だけに変換する。構造体は左右対称で安定しているため余分な垂直応力は発生しない。

　構造体には工業製品である合板パネルと木製の格子窓がはめ込まれている。

　主な空間は最上階にL字型に配されている。ガレージとプールは地面にじかに載ったコンクリートの床につくられている。またサービスエリアやキッチン，ダイニング，リビングルームは木構造の中にある。プールテラスはガレージのすぐ隣につくられている。例えば車を道路に停め，ガラスのスライドドアを開け放てばガレージをパーティのための囲われた空間として使うというようなこともできる。

Marcos Acayaba / Helio Olga House

Garage: view toward deck　ガレージ：デッキを見る

View from entrance toward dining/living area　玄関より食堂／居間方向を見る

View of garage from entrance area 玄関エリアからガレージを見る

Living room: looking west 居間：西を見る

Dining room 食堂

Living room: looking north　居間：北を見る

View toward kitchen from dining room　食堂から台所を見る

Marcos Acayaba / Helio Olga House

Staircase 階段室

Upward view of staircase 階段室見上げ

Playroom プレイルーム

Bedroom on northeast corner 北東隅部の寝室

Bathroom on bedroom level 寝室階の浴室

Pilotis of studio スタジオのピロティ

Marcos Acayaba / Helio Olga House

GESTO ARQUITETURA
JATOBÁ RESIDENCE
Santana de Parnaíba, São Paulo, Brazil

Photos: Yoshio Futagawa

Overall view from southeast 南東側全景

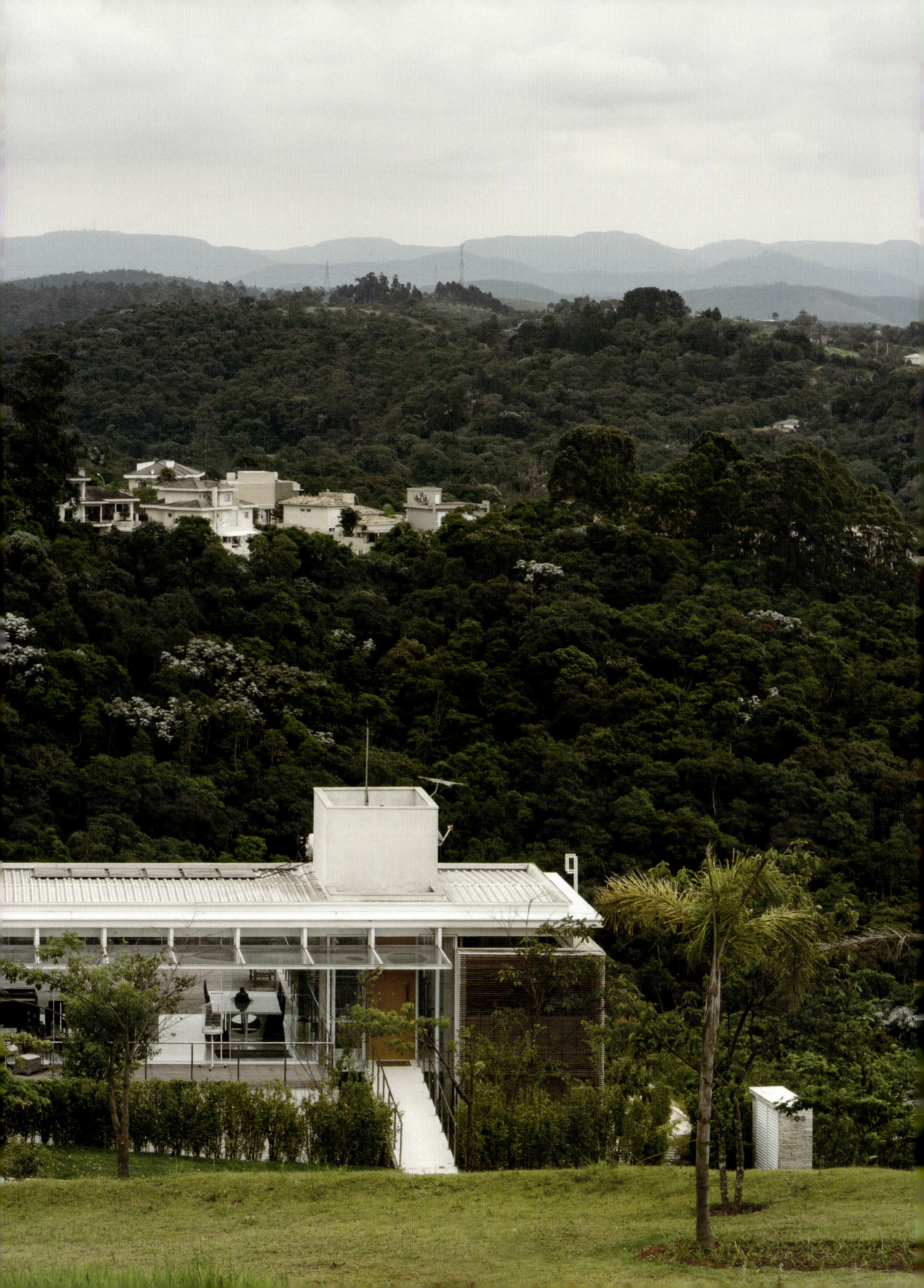

South view: deck and living room 南より見る：デッキと居間

Lower floor S=1:400

Ground floor

South elevation

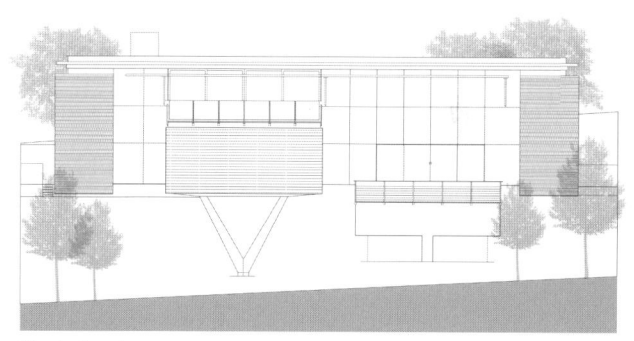

North elevation

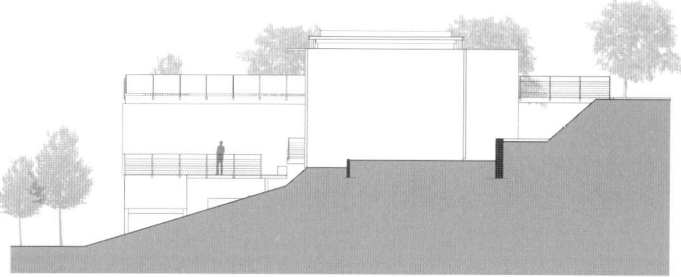

West elevation

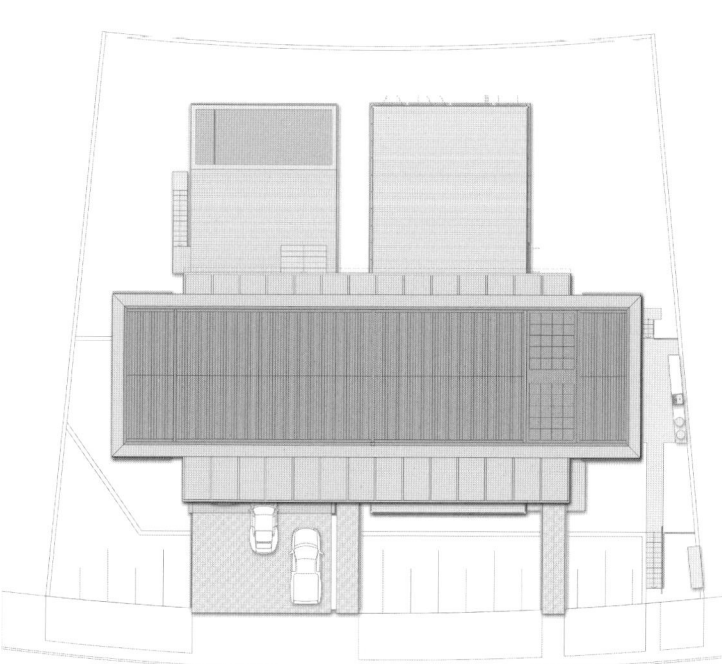

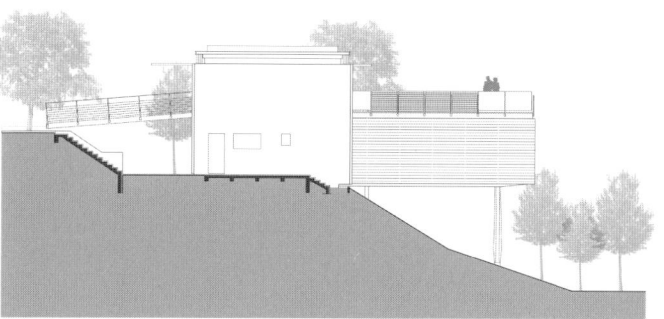

East elevation S=1:400

Roof

Gesto Arquitetura / Jatobá Residence   127

Entrance bridge 玄関のブリッジ

△Living room: looking east 居間：東を見る

View of living room from deck on north　北側のデッキより居間を見る▽

The Jatobá Residence is located in Santana do Parnaíba, a little and historical city in Metropolitan Region of São Paulo, where the natural landscape is very much preserved and the people can live together with some fragments of natural forest rounded by mountain chain and it is in this context and in a downhill ground that this residence is inserted.

The conception of this project have had as its primary purpose the maintenance of the landscape perception although the implementation of this constructed object in order to preserve the viewer connection for the visitors and the people who are walking in the street by the resulted small square place in front of the house.

Otherwise the internal space has organized into four independent and well-defined volumes connected and characterized by small transparent walkways or little bridges inside the house.

The result from this intervention reduced the vertical and horizontal distances between the blocks provides living spaces, cracks by passing the natural light and promoting external and internal visual through the building.

According to the owners resident it is possible to note the presence of people outside looking through the transparence as well as observing the residence and the landscape.

In addiction the intention of enabling the landscape view was the responsible for the organization of the internal space its use and distribution.

The architectural program provided living and working activities for a couple of movie director and producer so it includes all house uses and two offices with a little movie room.

The distribution of the activities inside allows scrolling through a path to the job by clearing separating the activities.

Walking by the building it is possible to share with collective public spaces like streets or squares in a city going through more collective and exposed areas in coexistence with the external and opened spaces while maintaining privacy.

Therefore we sought to provide contemplation in a direct relationship with the landscape through the house's transparences and the blocks that make up the built set are permeated with voids extending these spaces and fostering a sense of spaciousness.

Gesto Arquitetura / Jatobá Residence　129

Looking north from ground level: swimming pool below　地上レベルから北を見る：下にプール

Corridor on ground level: view toward living room　地上レベルの廊下：居間方向を見る

Double-height space facing wood deck on lower level: lift on center 下階，テラスに面した2層吹抜けのスペース：中央にはリフト

View from swimming pool on north 北側のプールから見る

Northeast corner 北東角部

Gesto Arquitetura / Jatobá Residence 133

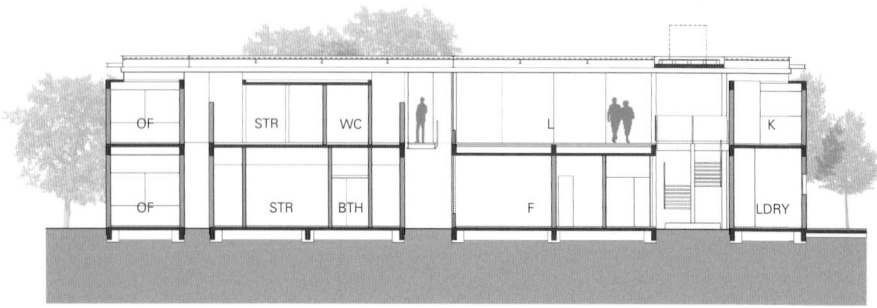

Longitudinal section

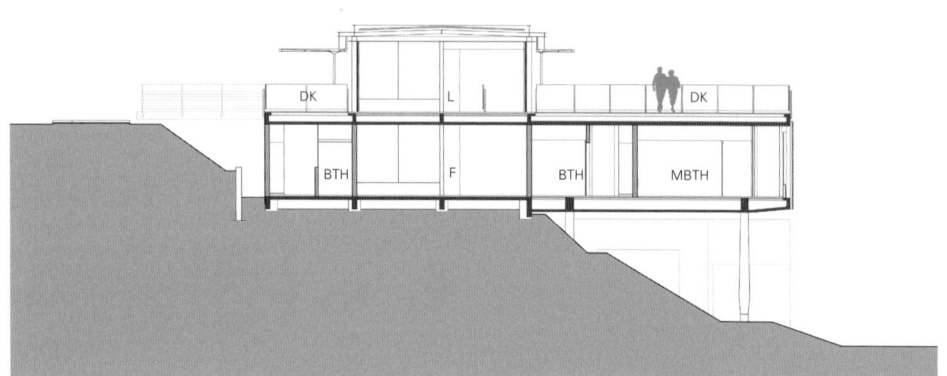

Cross section S=1:300

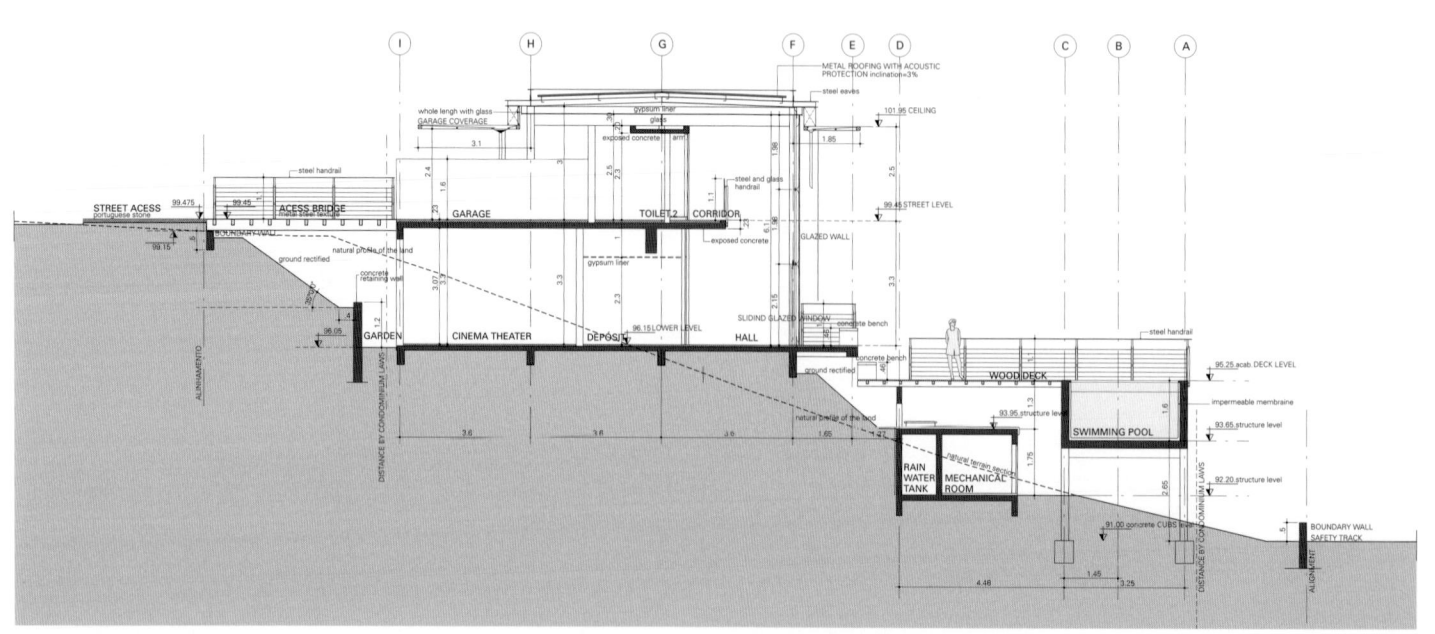

Sectional detail S=1:200

North elevation: view from deck on lower level　北面：下階のデッキより見る

　ジャトバ・ハウスはサンパウロ都市圏の古都サンタナ・デ・パルナイーバに位置している。山脈に囲まれた小さな都市では自然環境が良好に保たれ，自然林がいくつも点在し，人々と共生している。この住宅はそのようなコンテクストを背景として，傾斜した大地へと挿入される。

　この計画のコンセプトは，景観に対する認識を継承していくことに主眼を置いたものである。建物が建てられてもなお，来客や通りを行き交う人々が十分に眺望を得ることができるように，住宅の手前には小さな広場が計画された。

　その一方で，内部空間は明確に独立した四つのヴォリュームで構成され，各々が小さく透明な通路とブリッジで接続され特徴づけられている。

　このような操作の結果，ブロック同士を水平・垂直方向に近接して配置することで，リビングを構成し，スリットからは自然光が透過するとともに，内外の視線が建物を通り抜けるようになった。

　住宅のオーナーは外を行き交う通行人が透明な住宅を通して自然を眺めることができるようにと考えていた。

　また，内部空間の構成，利用，及び動線においても同様に，自然を眺めることができるようにする必要があった。

　この建築のプログラムは映画監督，及びプロデューサーである夫妻にリビングとワークスペースを提供するためのものである。そのため住宅としての全ての機能の他に，二つのオフィスと小規模の映写室が計画された。

　内部空間は様々な用途へと明確に区画された機能配置によって，まっすぐにワークスペースへと行くことができる。

　都市の街路や広場が屋外の共有空間を通して広がるように，建物に沿って歩いてゆくとパブリックスペースを共有することができる。そこでは屋外の開放的な空間が，プライバシーの守られた空間と共存している。

　それゆえに私たちは，住宅の透明性を通して自然との直接的な関係を計画に付与しようと考えた。建築全体を構成するブロックは，ヴォイドがその内部を貫通し，空間を拡張するとともに，広大な空間の獲得を促している。

Master bedroom　主寝室

Bedroom on south　南側の寝室

Washroom of bedroom on south　南側寝室の洗面室

Family room on lower level　下階，家族室

Architect: Gesto Arquitetura Ltda.—
Newton Massafumi Yamato,
Tânia Regina Parma, principals-in-charge;
Client: Mercedes and Cláudio Borreli
Consultant: Ycon Engenharia Ltda., structural; Projesp Engenharia Ltda., mechanical
General contractor:
Steel Construções e Empreendimentos Ltda.
Program: residence with a movie room
Structural system: steel, concrete structure
Major materials: wood, glass, steel, concrete
Site area: 986.80 m²
Built area: 612.70 m²
Total floor area: 450 m²
Design: 2010
Construction: 2011

Stairs to entrance　玄関への階段

Gesto Arquitetura / Jatobá Residence　137

REINACH MENDONÇA ARQUITETOS
MG RESIDENCE
São Paulo, São Paulo, Brazil
Photos: Yoshio Futagawa

View from swimming pool in garden 庭のスイミング・プールより見る

Garden with pools　プールのある庭

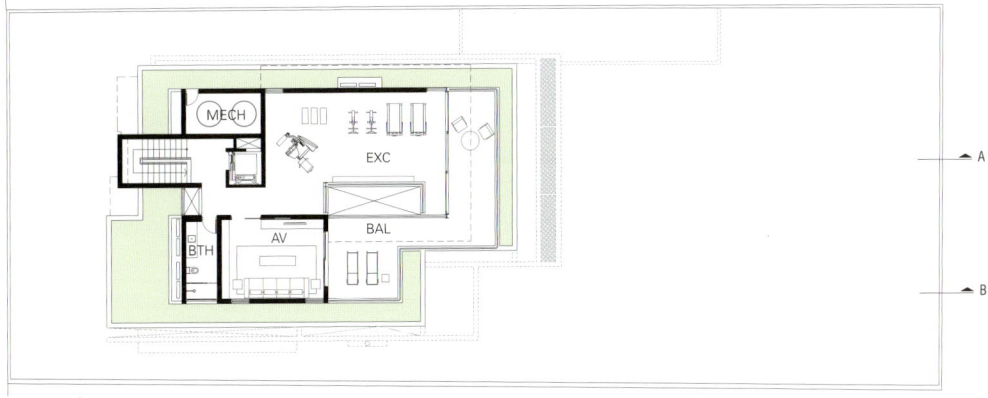

Second floor

First floor

Ground floor　S=1:400

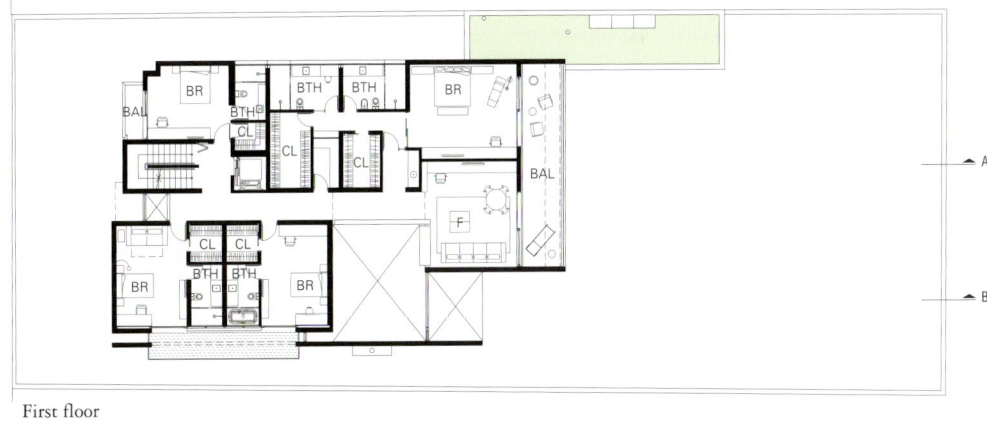

Reinach Mendonça Arquitetos / MG Residence　139

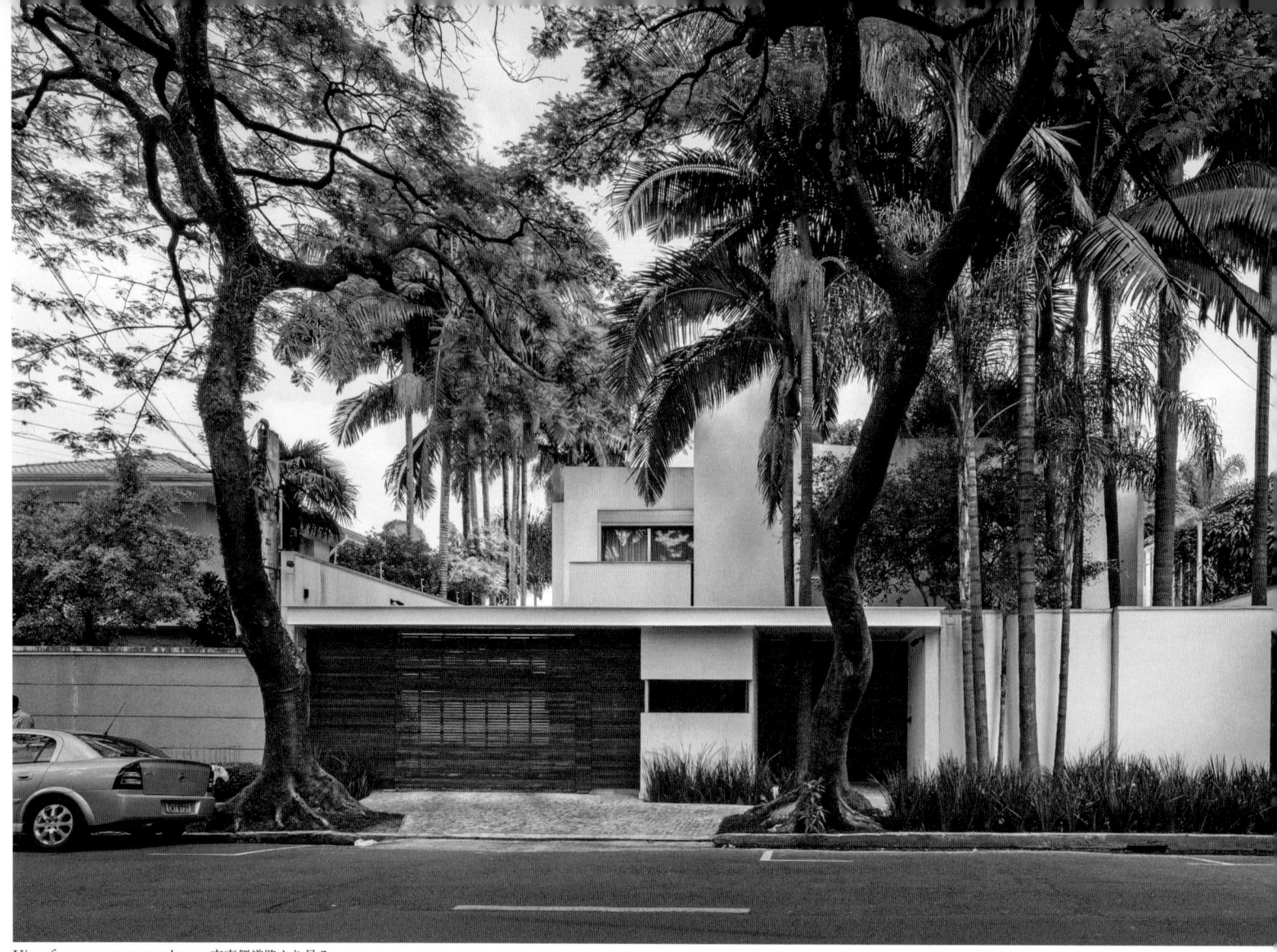

View from street on southeast 南東側道路より見る

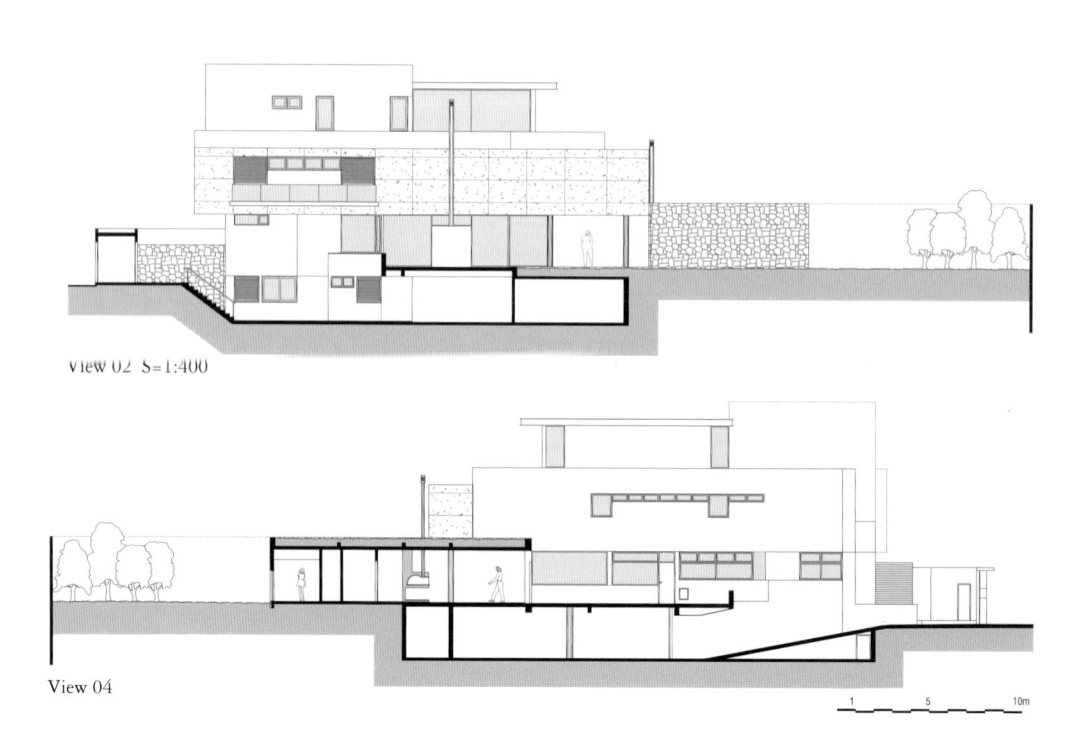

View 02 S=1:400

View 04

1 5 10m

Entrance 玄関

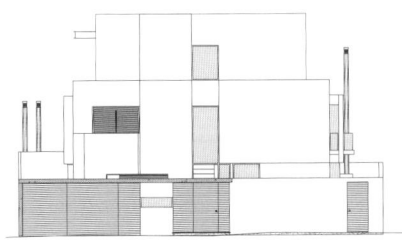

View 01

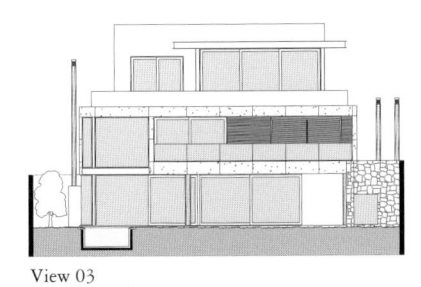

View 03

This residence, located in the upscale and wooded neighborhood area west of São Paulo, was deployed in a flat and deep site, with the main premise of making the most of existing green area at the back of the lot.

The environments are distributed on four floors including a basement, so that the extensive program could concentrate in a very compact area. On the ground level is just living area, facing the pool and a veranda, with the comfort of the shades of ancient trees that have been preserved.

Social spaces were turned toward the great garden in the background, used as security measure and privacy. A swimming pool with 25 meters laps, attends a family request that has swimming as sport.

The basement has an underground parking for 10 cars, which supplies the lack of free spaces in the surrounding streets. In it are also employee's dependencies—facing an "English gap"—and other technical areas of the house.

The architectural proposal, to keep people together and socializing, determines interconnected spaces even in the pool area. The laps partially invade the balcony of double height ceiling, integrated to the house atrium. The abundant presence of glass enables the person who is in the living room to see the daughter's room, the family room and dining room, while contemplating the garden and lap, talking to everyone. The atrium brings together all the environments, eliminating corridors and passageways. Abundant light entering the sides and roof, through successive small double height ceiling between floors, air and softens the program. The second floor, all glassed emanates light to the rest of the house.

The double height ceiling with glass panels, allows both, to look abroad and contact with the trees, and look for the interior and see the people moving through the house, turning circulations in open and pleasant spaces. The wide spans, the empty space inside, high ceilings and balconies helps air circulation, promoting cross ventilation and eliminating in most of the time, the use of air conditioning.

The structure, mixed concrete and steel, is part of a main box, a rectangular volume of concrete, streaky with metal beams. When switching the skeleton to a lighter material, we were able to relieve the structural system, making the party slim, with spans larger and lighter. In the second floor, which is more open, glazed and free, the structure is all in steel.

Living room: view toward garden 居間：庭を見る

サンパウロの西，緑豊かな高級住宅街に位置するこの住宅は，平坦で奥行きのある敷地に，その奥にあった緑地を最大限に活かすという前提のもとに建てられた。

地下を含めて4層の各階に空間が分配され，それによって巨大なプログラムを非常にコンパクトな面積に納めることが出来た。1階はプールとベランダに面したリビングのみで占められ，大切に育てられてきた古い木が心地よい木陰をつくる。

防犯とプライバシーの確保を兼ね，パブリック・スペースは大きな裏庭に向かって開かれている。趣味で水泳をする家族の希望で25メートルプールも設けられている。

地下には10台の車を収容できる地下駐車場があり，敷地周辺の通りの空きスペース不足を補っている。またここには「イングリッシュ・ギャップ（小さなドライエリア）」に面した使用人のための部屋と機械室などがある。

人々が集い交流するために，プールサイドも含めて相互に関係しあうような建築的空間の提案を行った。プールの一部が吹き抜けのバルコニーの方へと入り込み，家のアトリウムと一体となっている。またガラスを豊富に使うことで，リビングルームからプールや庭を眺めながら，同時に娘の部屋や家族室，ダイニングを見渡し会話もできる。アトリウムでは全ての空間が一つにまとめられ廊下や通路が姿を消している。家の屋根や側面から光を取り入れ，小さいながらも有効に機能する2層の高さの吹き抜けを通すことで建築プログラムを和らげることができる。3階部分はガラスで囲われ家の残りの部分に光を拡散させる。

吹き抜けにガラス窓を設けたことで，中から外の木を眺めることもでき，また室内を覗きこんで家の中を動き回る人々を見ることもできる。また同時に動線が開放的で快適な空間となる。大きく飛んだスパンや開放的な空間，また高い天井とバルコニーは，室内の空気循環を助け，通風を促し，冷暖房を使用することはほぼない。

構造はコンクリートと鉄骨の混構造で，鉄骨の梁で縞模様になったメインの長方形のコンクリートボックスと一体化されている。スケルトン部分を軽量な素材に変更したことで構造の負荷を軽減し，スパンをより長く軽快なものにすることができた。3階は全て鉄骨とガラスで出来ているためさらに自由で開放的である。

Reinach Mendonça Arquitetos / MG Residence

Living room: dining room and patio on right　居間：右奥に食堂とパティオ

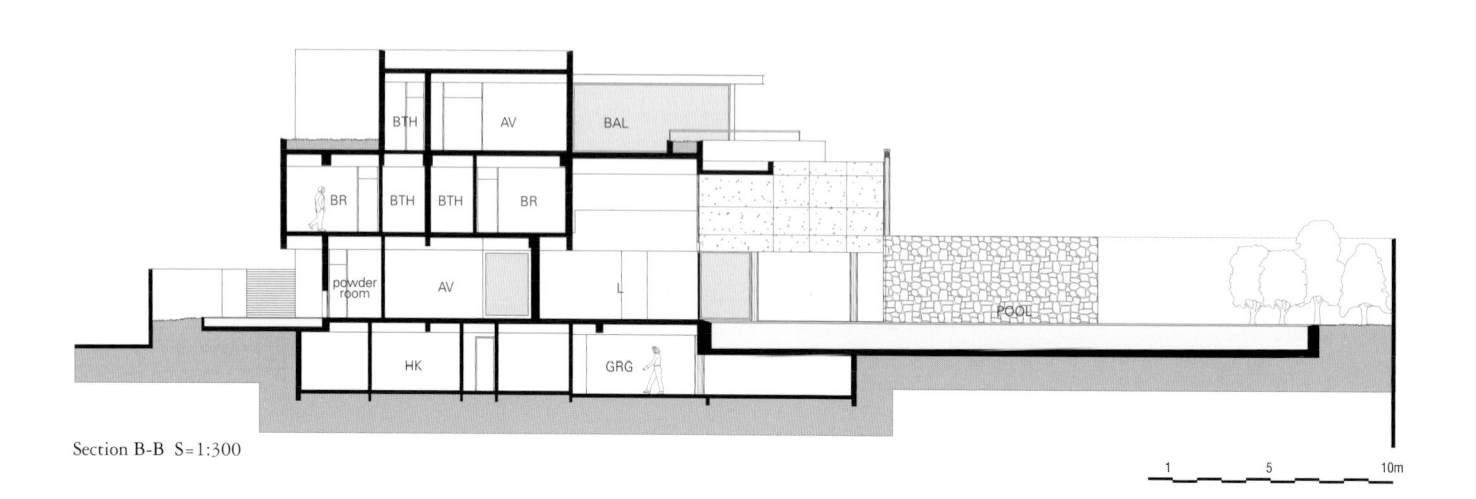

Section B-B S=1:300

Downward view of living room 居間見下ろし

Dining room 食堂

Exercise room on second floor　3階，エクササイズ・ルーム

Balcony on first floor　2階，バルコニー

View toward family room on first floor
2階，家族室を見る

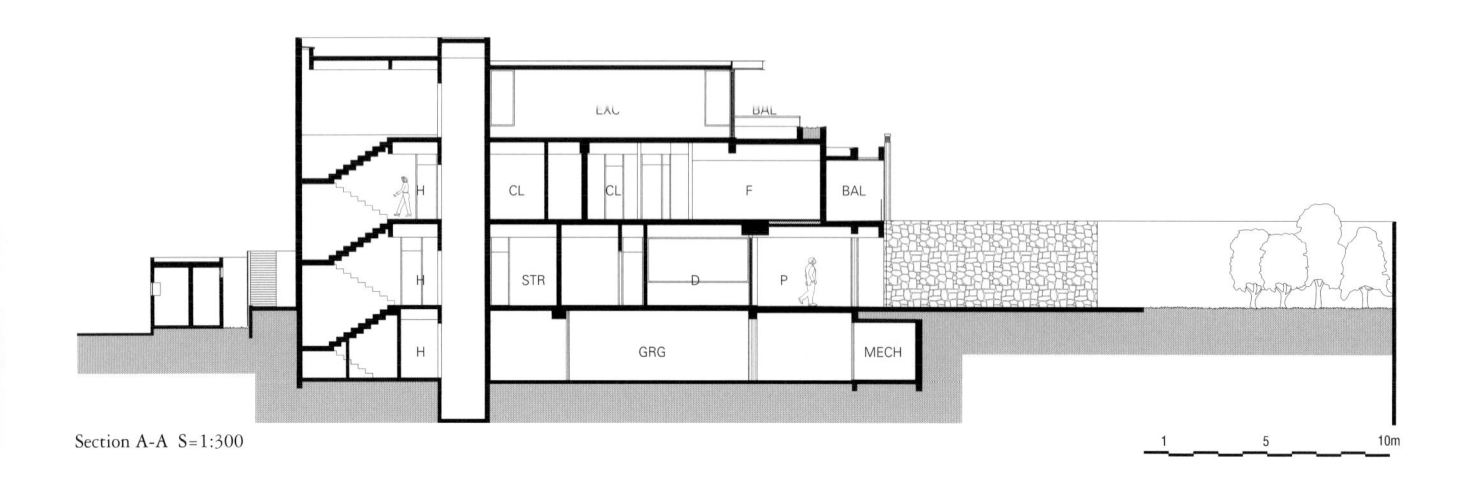

Section A-A　S=1:300

Architect: Reinach Mendonça Arquitetos Associados—Henrique Reinach, Mauricio Mendonça, principals-in-charge; Marcelo Zahr, Frederico Zara Chiarelli, Luciana Maki, Humberto Buso, Tony Chen, Flora Fujii, Lucas Padovani, Mauricio Metello, Maíra Cordeiro, Flávia Henriques, Natália Campos, Ana Júlia Sprovieri, Natasha Villaça, project team
Consultant: SVS Projetos Estruturais Mechanical, structural; Rewald Engenharia, engineer; RAP Arquitetura, interior designer; Martha Gavião Arquitetura Paisagística, landscape
General contractor: JZM Planejamento Imobiliário e Construção
Program: single-family residence
Structural system: mixed concrete, steel structure
Major materials: exposed concrete, stone, glass
Site area: 1,029 m²
Built area: 380 m²
Total floor area: 1,350 m²
Design: 2008-09
Construction: 2008-12

Sauna サウナ

ANDRADE MORETTIN
FS HOUSE
Avaré, São Paulo, Brazil

Photos: Yoshio Futagawa

Overall view from reservoir 貯水池からの全景

Ground floor S=1:500

Section C

Southeast elevation

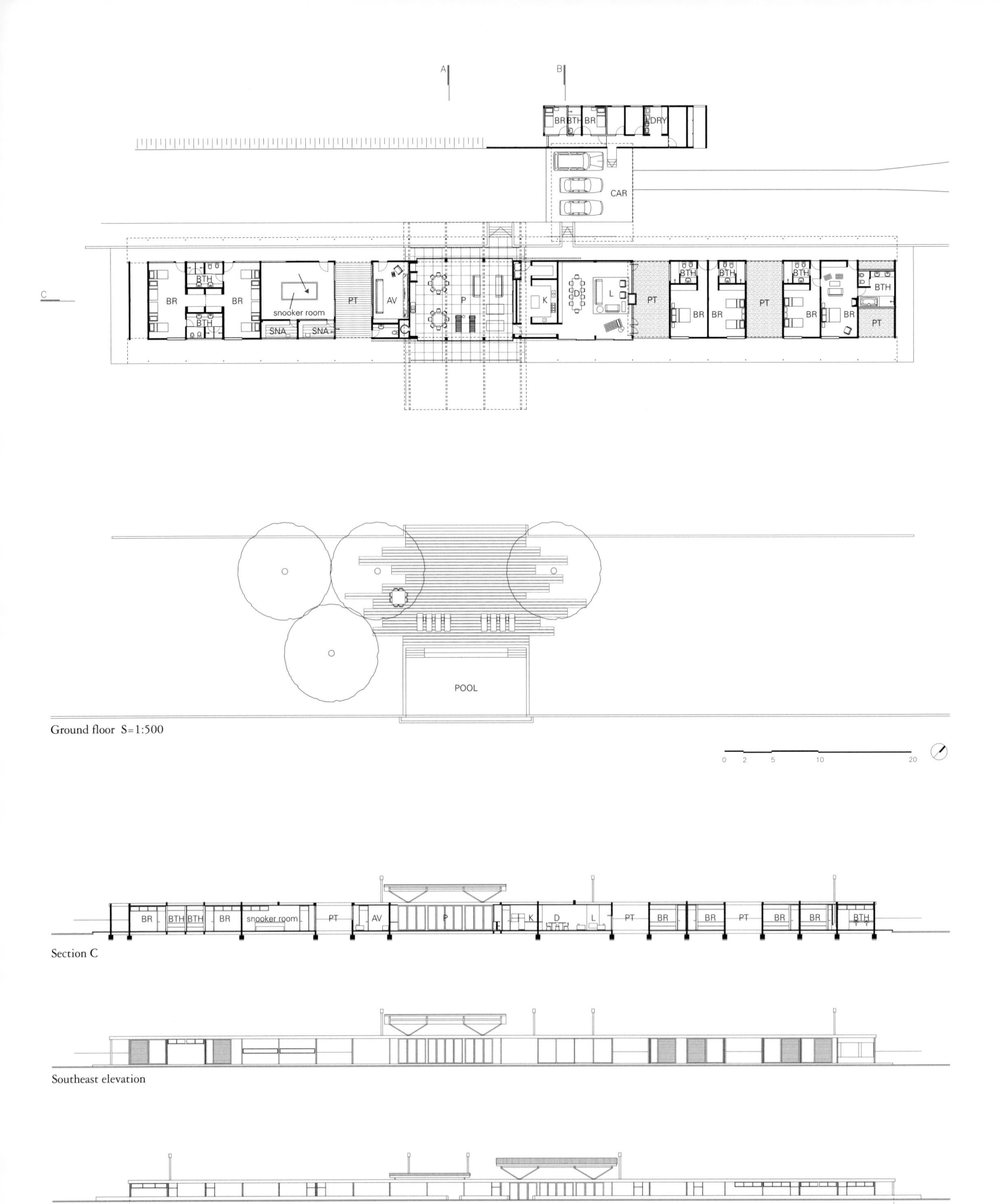

Northwest elevation S=1:500

Site plan S=1:8000

Southwest elevation

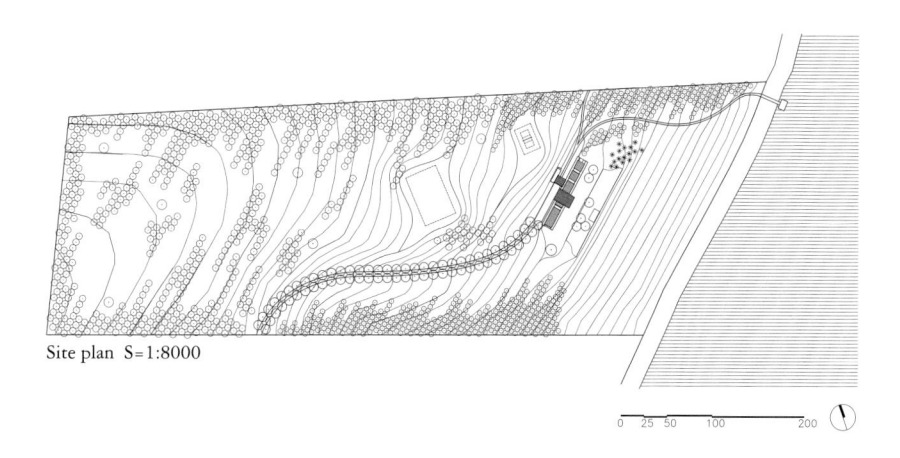

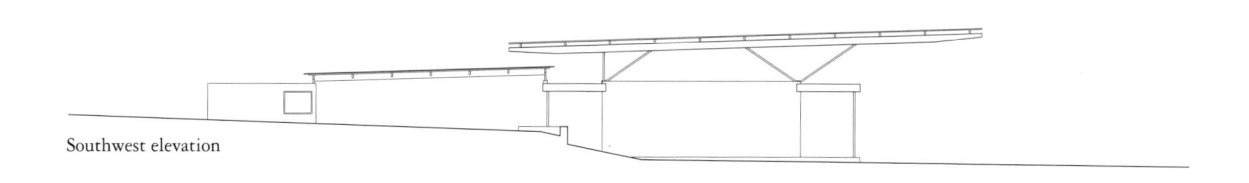

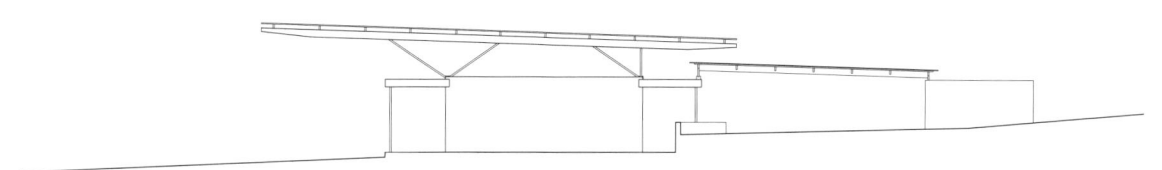

Northeast elevation

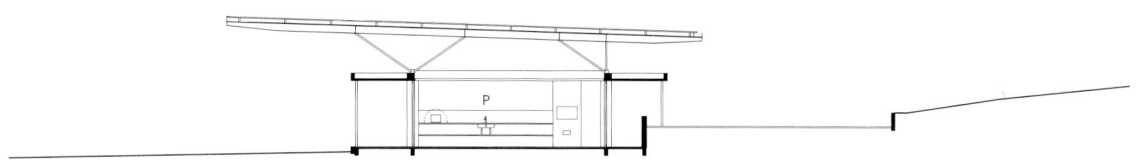

Section A

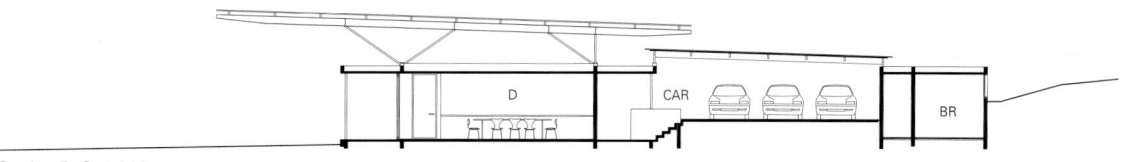

Section B S=1:300

Andrade Morettin / FS House   151

View from east 東より見る

View toward swimming pool and reservoir プールと貯水池を見る

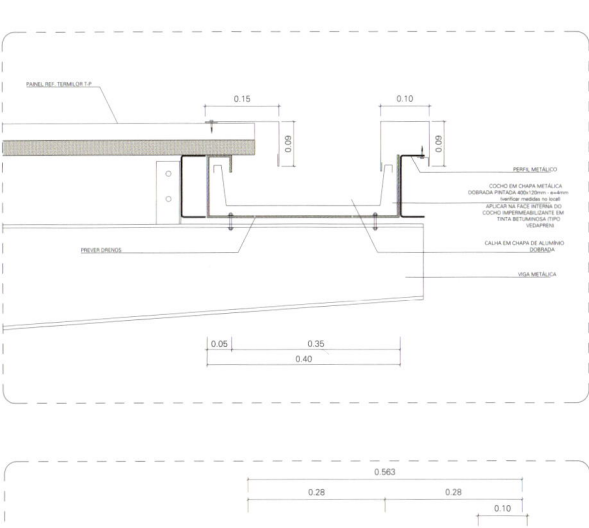

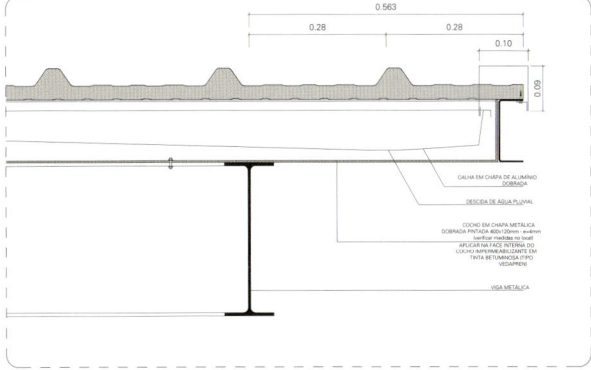

Details S=1:15

Patio パティオ

Andrade Morettin / FS House

View from entrance on northwest　北西側の玄関より見る

Entrance (right) and porch (semi outdoor living area)　玄関（右）とポーチ（半屋外の居間エリア）

Semi outdoor living area 半屋外の居間エリア

Semi outdoor living area: view toward reservoir 半屋外の居間エリア：貯水池を見る

The residence is located on a large property, on the shore of the Avaré reservoir, 250 km from São Paulo. The vastness of the landscape, characterized by scarce vegetation, suggested a discreet implantation.

The house is a long single-floor pavilion that is inserted into the landscape as a horizontal line. This line is disturbed only by a great roof structure that, hovering above the pavilion, suggests the presence of a special place: a large covered terrace which is also the point of entry and central meeting place of the house.

The spatial structure of the house is determined by its cross section. Two long concrete structures stretch along the entire length of the house determining the position of the longitudinal circulation and of the balcony looking out on the lake. These structures simultaneously serve as support for the roofs of the enclosed volumes, collect rainwater and provide shade.

Connected by the two longitudinal structures, the enclosed volumes shelter the more private activities of the house, such as bedrooms and bathrooms. In the central area of the house, under the big roof structure, the collective activities such as the porch, the living room and the kitchen are concentrated.

The living spaces and circulations of the house are open, taking maximum advantage of the mild local climate and the permanent views that the place offers.

Patio. Living room on left　パティオ。左は居間

Living room　居間

この住宅はサンパウロから250キロ離れたアバレの貯水池の浜辺に面し、広大な所有地の中に計画された。荒涼とした植生の広がる遠大な風景からは、控え目な建築が連想された。

　計画は平屋の細長い住宅である。これが1本の直線として風景の中へと挿入される。直線を遮るのは1枚の巨大な屋根である。屋根は建築の上空に浮かび、そこが特別な場所であるということを示している。天蓋によって覆われたこのテラスはエントランスとして、また、同時に人の集まる場所としての役割を担う。

　この住宅の空間構造は、断面計画によって決定されている。二つの細長いコンクリート構造が住宅の全長にわたって延びる。この構造が縦軸動線と、湖を望むバルコニーの配置計画を決定している。これらの構造は閉じられたヴォリュームの屋根を支持すると共に、雨水を集め、日除けとしての役割を果たす。

　閉じられたヴォリューム同士は2本の縦軸構造によって結ばれ、寝室や浴室といった住宅のプライベートな機能が収容されている。住宅中央部の大屋根の下にはエントランス・ポーチ、リビング、及びキッチンが、共有部として集約して配置されている。

　この住宅では動線とリビングを外部に向けて開放することで、この地域の温暖な気候とその土地のいつまでも変わらない風景の魅力を引き出している。

Bedroom 寝室

Bathroom 浴室

Architect: Andrade Morettin Arquitetos—
Vinicius Andrade, Marcelo Morettin, principals-in-charge;
Marina Mermelstein, Marcio Tanaka, Marcelo Maia Rosa, Merten Nefs, Renata Andrulis, Thiago Natal Duarte, project team
Client: Felipe Sigrist
Consultant: Aiello Engenharia, structural; KML, installations;
Isabel Duprat Arquitetura Paisagítica, landscape; Reka iluminação, lighting
Structural system: reinforced concrete
Major materials: concrete blocks
Site area: 175,000 m²
Built area: 1,045 m²
Total floor area: 1,045 m²
Design: 2006
Construction: 2007-09

Bedroom 寝室

Andrade Morettin / FS House

GA DOCUMENT
Global Architecture

GA DOCUMENT presents the finest in international design, focusing on architectures that expresses our times and striving to record the history of contemporary architecture. International scholars and critics provide insightful texts to further inform the reader of the most up-to-date ideas and events in the profession.

多様に広がり、変化を見せる世界の現代建築の動向をデザインの問題を中心に取り上げ、現代建築の完全な記録をめざしつつ、時代の流れに柔軟に対応した独自の視点から作品をセレクションし、新鮮な情報を世界に向けて発信する唯一のグローバルな建築専門誌。

English and Japanese text, Size: 300×257mm

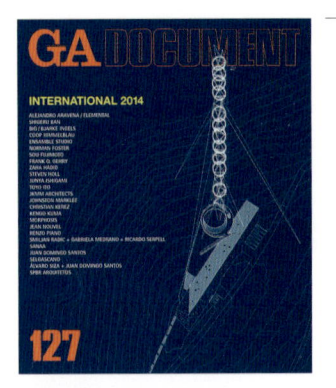

---

127 Latest Issue
180 pages, 96 in color
¥3,200

Special Issue: "INTERNATIONAL 2014"
特集：第22回〈現代世界の建築家〉展

Projects:
Alejandro Aravena/ELEMENTAL | Shigeru Ban | BIG/Bjarke Ingels | Coop Himmelblau | Ensamble Studio | Norman Foster | Sou Fujimoto | Frank O. Gehry | Zaha Hadid | Steven Holl | Junya Ishigami | Toyo Ito | JKKM Architects | Johnston Marklee | Christian Kerez | Kengo Kuma | Morphosis | Jean Nouvel | Renzo Piano | Smiljan Radic + Gabriela Medrano + Ricardo Serpell | SANAA | Juan Doming Santos | selgascano | Álvaro Siza + Juan Doming Santos | SPBR Arquitetos

---

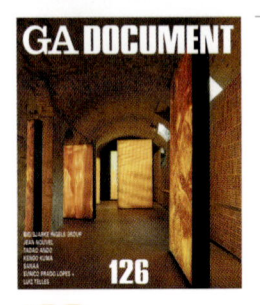

126
144 pages, 84 in color
¥3,200

Works:
BIG / Danish Maritime Museum | Jean Nouvel / Doha Tower | Tadao Ando / Hansol Museum | Kengo Kuma / Besançon City Arts and Culture Center | SANAA / Junko Fukutake Hall (Okayama Univ. J-Hall) | and others
Treasure of Architecture: Eurico Prado Lopes + Luiz Telles / CCSP—Centro Cultural São Paulo

作品：
BIG／デンマーク海洋博物館｜ジャン・ヌヴェル／ドーハ・タワー、ファブリカ・モリッツ・バルセロナ｜安藤忠雄／ハンソル・ミュージアム｜隈研吾／ブザンソン芸術文化センター｜SANAA／Junko Fukutake Hall, 他
名作建築を訪ねて：
エウリコ・プラド・ロペス＋ルイス・テレース／サンパウロ文化センター（CCSP）

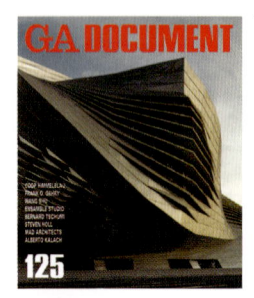

125
144 pages, 90 in color
¥3,200

Works:
Coop Himmelblau / Dalian International Conference Center | Wang Shu / Tiles Hill—New Reception Center in Xiangshan Campus, China Academy of Art | S. Holl / Campbell Sports Center | MAD Architects / China Wood Sculpture Museum | A. Kalach / Reforma 27 | and others
Projects:
Frank O. Gehry, Steven Holl

作品：
コープ・ヒンメルブラウ／大連国際コンファレンス・センター｜ワン・シュウ／瓦山―中国美術学院象山キャンパス、レセプション棟｜S・ホール／キャンベル・スポーツ・センター｜MADアーキテクツ／中国木彫美術館｜A・カラチ／レフォルマ27, 他
プロジェクト：
フランク・O・ゲーリー、スティーヴン・ホール

124
204 pages, 120 in color
¥3,200

Special Issue: "INTERNATIONAL 2013"
特集：第21回〈現代世界の建築家〉展

Projects:
Alejandro Aravena/ELEMENTAL | BIG/Bjarke Ingels | Tatiana Bilbao | Iñaqui Carnicero | CJ Lim/Studio 8 Architects | Delugan Meissl | Ensamble Studio | Sou Fujimoto | Grupo SP | JKMM Architects | Johnston Marklee | Christian Kerez | Kengo Kuma | MAD Architects | Michael Maltzan | MVRDV | Njiric+ Arhitekti | O'Donnell Tuomey | Smiljan Radic + Eduardo Castillo | Fernando Romero | SANAA | selgascano + hochrein_architekten | SPBR Arquitetos | Wolfgang Tschapeller | UNStudio

---

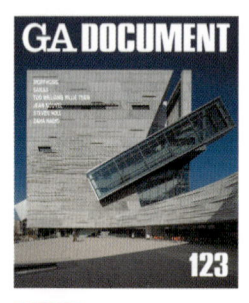

123
144 pages, 84 in color
¥3,200

Works:
Morphosis / Perot Museum of Nature and Science | SANAA / Louvre-Lens | T. Williams B. Tsien / Reva and David Logan Center for the Arts, University of Chicago | J. Nouvel / Theater of Archipelago, Perpignan | S. Holl / Raffles City Chengdu—Sliced Porosity Block | Z. Hadid / Galaxy SOHO, Beijing; Pierres-Vives | and others
Projects: Morphosis

作品：
モーフォシス／ペロー自然科学博物館｜SANAA／ルーヴル・ランス｜T・ウィリアムズ B・ツィン／シカゴ大学、レア＆デイヴィッド・ローガン・アートセンター｜J・ヌヴェル／ペルピニャン・アーケペラゴ・シアター｜S・ホール／ラッフルズ・シティー成都｜Z・ハディド／望京SOHO、ピエール=ヴィーヴ、他

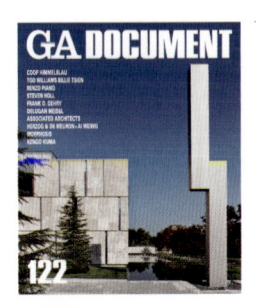

122
144 pages, 90 in color
¥3,200

Works:
Coop Himmelblau / Busan Cinema Center | TWBT / Barnes Foundation—New Philadelphia Campus | F. O. Gehry / Hong Kong Residential | Herzog & de Meuron and Ai Weiwei / Serpentine Gallery Pavilion 2012 | K. Kuma / Xinjin Zhi Museum | and others
Projects: Steven Holl, Morphosis

作品：
コープ・ヒンメルブラウ／釜山シネマセンター、釜山国際映画祭会場｜TWBT／新フィラデルフィア・キャンパス、バーンズ・ファンデーション｜R・ピアノ／ロンシャン・ゲートハウス＋修道院｜F・O・ゲーリー／香港レジデンシャル｜デルガン・マイスル／アイ・フィルム・インスティテュート, 他
プロジェクト：スティーヴン・ホール、モーフォシス

121
204 pages, 114 in color
¥3,200

Special Issue: "INTERNATIONAL 2012"
特集：第20回〈現代世界の建築家〉展

Projects:
AZL/Zhang Lei | Alejandro Aravena | BIG/Bjarke Ingels | Iñaqui Carnicero | Delugan Meissl | Sou Fujimoto | Antón García-Abril | Grupo SP | Christian Kerez | Kengo Kuma | Michael Maltzan | Mansilla+Tuñón | MVRDV | Hrvoje Njiric | O'Donnell+Tuomey | Smiljan Radic | Michel Rojkind | SANAA | selgascano | Fran Silvestre | Snøhetta | SPBR arquitetos | Studio 8/CJ Lim | Wolfgang Tschapeller | UNStudio | Urbanus | Wang Shu

---

表記価格に消費税は含まれておりません。